11/76

10536

Date Due

DEC 1 3 1976		
MAY 3 0 1978		
SEP 2 3 1978		
OCT 18 1982		
NOV 8		
DEC 1 3 1990		

TAKEN BY THE INDIANS

TAKEN BY THE INDIANS

TRUE TALES OF CAPTIVITY

ALICE DICKINSON

Franklin Watts   New York   London   1976

Photographs courtesy of:

The New York Public Library Picture Collection: 6, 10, 21, 29, 56, 92, 99; The American Museum of Natural History: 24, 77; Denver Public Library, Western History Department: 42, 112; The New-York Historical Society, New York City: 46; Genesee State Park and Recreation Commission: 64; Collections of the Michigan History Division: 67; Royal Ontario Museum, Toronto, Canada: 71; Superior Publishing Company, *Photographers of the Frontier West*, by Ralph Andrews: 103; National Collection of Fine Arts, Smithsonian Institution: 118, 123; U.S. Signal Corps in The National Archives: 129.

Library of Congress Cataloging in Publication Data

Dickinson, Alice.
　　Taken by the Indians.

　　Bibliography: p.
　　Includes index.
　　SUMMARY: Narrates the captivities of three women and three men by North American Indians during 1676 to 1864 using excerpts from their original accounts.
　　1. Indians of North America—Captivities—Juvenile literature. [1. Indians of North America—Captivities] I. Title.
E85.D52　　973'.04'97　　75-22307
ISBN 0-531-01107-0

CONTENTS

INTRODUCTION

"Captured by the Indians"—today these words carry an atmosphere of fiction and romance. Yet only a century ago there were countless men and women who had experienced the realities of Indian captivity and returned to tell of their adventures. Even more did not return. It will never be known how many white captives died or were murdered by their captors. Nor will anyone ever know how many captives chose to stay among the Indians, and quietly disappeared into tribal life. For many, even some of those who returned, the Indians and their way of living had great appeal. If they were captured in infancy, it was the only life they knew.

From almost the beginning of European settlement of North America, the Indians took white captives. Sometimes these captives were seized in warfare; sometimes they were taken in retribution because Indians had been captured and sold into slavery; sometimes they were taken to replace Indians who had died in battle or by disease. Among the tribes a helping hand was always welcome, and the captives—especially if they were young and healthy and of a pleasant disposition—were often adopted into the tribes. In many cases, those who were so accepted by the Indians found a congenial place for themselves. For other captives, assigned to slavery, life was not so pleasant.

The captives stayed for varying lengths of time among the Indians. John Tanner, adopted by tribesmen, lived for almost thirty years among them. Mary Rowlandson spent eleven and one half weeks in slavery to an Indian chief. Some of the captives returned and resumed their lives without attempting to record their experiences, but a surprising number did set down their recollections. Their stories give us a matchless firsthand view of earlier America and its history. Many of the captives were good observers with a keen ability to capture a scene or an incident in words. In the narratives of captivity there are detailed descriptions of Indian dress and customs, word portraits of individuals, and a perhaps unparalleled view of the North American continent, wilderness and prairie, as it was in those days—magnificent, unspoiled, and rich in plant and animal life. Many of the captives traveled hundreds of miles with the Indians, often on foot, and they never forgot what they had seen.

The narratives have some things in common. One is a preoccupation with food. For the Indians, even those who were agriculturists, game was an important item. When game was scarce, starvation might follow. The day-to-day problems of food supply worried captives as well as captors.

Another subject encountered again and again in the captives' accounts is the deadly effect of the white man's culture on the Indians. In particular, alcohol and diseases brought by the settlers took their toll.

Rights of ownership of a captured person seem to have been much the same among the tribes. When a white person was seized, he belonged to the Indian who first took him. However, he was often sold or given to someone in the tribe who had lost a relative by death. This person could do with the captive as he wished—kill him, or adopt him to take the departed relative's place. Adoption was often preferred.

All the captives saw cruelty and torture by the Indians, even though they themselves may have been kindly treated. They recognized that the Indians' harsh treatment of enemies was the same whether the enemies were white or Indian. Many of the captives freely admitted that the settlers were equally vicious in their treatment of the tribesmen. In her account of captivity among the Sioux, Fanny Kelly tells of seeing Indians die from eating crackers soaked in strychnine, which had purposely been placed along the wagon trails by westward pioneers.

This book contains the stories of six captives, three women and three men, extending over a period of time from 1676 to 1864. As far as space permits, their own narratives are quoted. Though they shared the prejudices of their day, viewing the Indians as savages to be feared, it is notable how often in these narratives we see the captives being gradually won over to a different point of view, until they came to understand their captors and to view them with friendship and affection.

MARY ROWLANDSON

Mary Rowlandson's captivity took place in Massachusetts Colony in 1676, during King Philip's War, a fierce conflict between the colonists and some of the local tribes.

The earliest settlers in the Massachusetts Bay and Plymouth colonies had been determined that their relations with the Indians should be friendly, and so they were for some years. The Indians offered invaluable help to the colonists during their first days in America. In time, the new settlers established trade with the Indians and furnished them with tools and other goods on which the Indians came to depend.

Friendly as the English colonists' attitude may have been, it was colored by a feeling of superiority. The newcomers could not see the Indians as equal persons of a separate culture that was right for them, but thought of the native Americans as "heathens" and "savages." In part, this viewpoint was due to the colonists' Puritan belief, which, they were firmly convinced, was God's one true way. They dreamed of winning over the Indians to their religion and way of life. Some headway was made in this direction when John Eliot and other missionaries succeeded in converting some of the Indians to Christianity. These converts were known as praying Indians.

As the Indians became more and more dependent on British goods, as the number of colonists and their demands for land increased, and as some of the Indians adopted English ways of living, many tribal members began to feel concern about the future. The more thoughtful New England Indians foresaw that in time they would be engulfed by the ever more powerful English colonists.

In the early 1670s, King Philip, chief of the Wampanoags, determined to seek alliances among the tribes for the purpose of pushing the English out of the territory before it was too late. When an Indian informer warned the colonists of Philip's intentions, circumstances forced the chief and his allies into a war before they were fully prepared for it.

Not all the tribes joined with Philip, and his effort was doomed from the start. The colonists were slow to react, however, and at first their attempts at defense were clumsy. Massachusetts Bay Colony at this time consisted of a string of settlements along the coast, and outer rings of towns dotted here and there in the deep forest and connected only by trails. These outer settlements took the worst of the Indians' fury. The dawn attack, with the firing of houses and the slaughter or capture of inhabitants, became a dreaded possibility that all too often came true. Mrs. Mary Rowlandson gives us a vivid description of one such attack, that on Lancaster where she lived. Her husband, the town's clergyman, was away from home at the time and neighbors, fearing an Indian onslaught, had turned her house into one of a number of garrisons in which they took refuge. This house was the only one in Lancaster that was captured by the Indians, although the town was later temporarily abandoned.

Mrs. Rowlandson remained in captivity as a slave for eleven and one half weeks. During this time she shared the life of the Indians as, starving and cold and driven from their usual winter quarters, they were harried through the wilderness by the colonial troops. First published in 1682, her record of captivity has survived as a remarkable piece of historical writing and a revealing self-portrait of a Puritan woman who was truly sustained by the faith in God which her religion had taught her.

Although Mrs. Rowlandson, in referring to the Indians, uses

King Philip's efforts to drive out the colonists ended in his death.

the clichés of her time—heathen, savages, barbarians—her liking and understanding of these people appear to have increased during her time with them. She especially expresses gratitude to her Indian master for his treatment of her; she makes no effort to hide her dislike for his wife, her mistress, but this seems to have been a matter of clashing personalities. Mary Rowlandson also gives us an extremely human portrayal of King Philip, with whom she became acquainted.

Mary Rowlandson was impressed by the Indians' ability to survive under great stress. During all the time she was with them she saw no one die of hunger, although often everyone was in desperate straits for food. "Their chief food was groundnuts," she writes. "They eat also nuts and acorns, artichokes, lily roots, ground beans, and several other weeds and roots that I know not. They would pick up old bones, and cut them in pieces at the joints, and if they were full of worms and maggots they would scald them over the fire, to make the vermin come out, and then boil them, and drink up the liquor, and then beat the great ends of them in a mortar, and so eat them. They would eat horses' guts and ears, and all sorts of wild birds which they could catch; also bear, venison, beavers, tortoise, frogs, squirrels, dogs, skunks, rattlesnakes, yea the very bark of trees; besides all sorts of creatures and provisions which they plundered from the English."

Mary Rowlandson was obviously a woman of great stamina and adaptability—qualities for which the Indians appear to have respected her. Excerpts from her *A Narrative of Captivity* follow.

On the 10th of February, 1676, came the Indians with great numbers upon Lancaster: their first coming was about sunrising. Hearing the noise of some guns, we looked out; several houses were burning, and smoke ascending to heaven. There were five persons taken in one house; the father and mother and a sucking child they [the Indians] knocked on the head, the other two they took and carried away alive. There are two others who, being out of their garrison upon occasion, were set upon; one was knocked on the head, the other escaped. Another there was who, running along, was shot and wounded, and fell down; he begged of them his life, promising them money, as they told me, but they would not hearken to him, but knocked him on the head, stripped him naked, and split open his bowels. Another, seeing many of the Indians about his barn, ventured and went out, but was quickly shot down. There were three others belonging to the same garrison who were killed. . . .

At length they came and beset our house, and quickly it was the dolefulest day that ever mine eyes saw. The house stood upon the edge of a hill; some of the Indians got behind the hill, others into the barn, and others behind anything that would shelter them; from all which places they shot against the house, so that the bullets seemed to fly like hail, and quickly they wounded one man among us, then another, and then a third. About two hours, according to my observation in that amazing time, they had been about the house before they prevailed to

fire it, which they did with flax and hemp which they brought
out of the barn. . . .

Some in our house were fighting for their lives, others wal-
lowing in blood, the house on fire over our heads, and the
bloody heathen ready to knock us on the head if we stirred out.
. . . Then I took my children, and one of my sisters [Mrs.
Drew] hers to go forth and leave the house, but as soon as we
came to the door and appeared, the Indians shot so thick that
the bullets rattled against the house as if one had taken a handful of stones and threw them, so that we were forced to give
back. . . . But out we must go, the fire increasing and coming
along behind us roaring, and the Indians gaping before us with
their guns, spears, and hatchets to devour us. . . . The bullets
flying thick, one went through my side, and the same, as would
seem, through the bowels and hand of my poor child in my
arms. . . . The Indians laid hold of us, pulling me one way and
the children another, and said, "Come, go along with us." I told
them they would kill me; they answered, if I were willing to go
along with them they would not hurt me.

Of the thirty-seven persons in this house, one escaped,
twelve were killed, and twenty-four were taken captive. Mrs.
Rowlandson had often said that if the Indians should come, she
would prefer death to captivity, but when the time arrived, their
"glittering weapons" so daunted her spirit that she chose to go
with her captors rather than end her days then and there.

About a mile we went that night, up upon a hill, within sight of
the town, where we intended to lodge. . . . Oh, the roaring, and
singing, and dancing, and yelling of those black creatures in the
night, which made the place a lively resemblance of hell. And
miserable was the waste that was there made of horses, cattle,
sheep, swine, calves, lambs, roasting pigs, and fowls (which they
had plundered in the town), some roasting, some lying and
burning, and some boiling, to feed our merciless enemies who
were joyful enough, though we were disconsolate. To add to the
dolefulness of the former day and the dismalness of the present
night, my thoughts ran upon my losses and sad, bereaved condition. All was gone, my husband gone (at least separated from
me, he being in the Bay [Boston]; and to add to my grief, the
Indians told me they would kill him as he came homeward),

my children gone, my relations and friends gone, our house and home, and all our comforts within door and without, all was gone (except my life, and I knew not but the next moment that might go too).

There remained nothing to me but one poor wounded babe, and it seemed at present worse than death, that it was in such a pitiful condition, bespeaking compassion, and I had no refreshing for it, nor suitable things to revive it. . . .

But now (the next morning), I must turn my back upon the town and travel with them into the vast and desolate wilderness, I knew not whither. It is not my tongue or pen can express the sorrows of my heart and bitterness of my spirit that I had at this departure. . . . One of the Indians carried my poor wounded babe upon a horse; it went moaning all along, "I shall die, I shall die." I went on foot after it with sorrow that cannot be expressed. At length I took it off the horse and carried it in my arms, till my strength failed and I fell down with it. Then they set me upon a horse with my wounded child in my lap, and there being no furniture [saddle] on the horse's back, as we were going down a steep hill we both fell over the horse's head, at which they, like inhuman creatures, laughed. . . .

After this it quickly began to snow, and when night came on they stopped. And now down I must sit in the snow, by a little fire, and a few boughs behind me, with my sick child in my lap, and calling much for water, being now, through the wound, fallen into a violent fever; my own wound, also growing so stiff that I could scarce sit down or rise up. . . .

The morning being come, they prepared to go on their way; one of the Indians got upon a horse, and they sat me up behind him, with my poor sick babe in my lap. . . . This day in the afternoon, about an hour by sun, we came to the place where they intended, viz., an Indian town called Wenimesset, northward of Quabaug [Brookfield]. . . . The next day was the Sabbath. . . . This day there came to me one Robert Pepper, a man belonging to Roxbury, who was taken at Capt. Beers' fight, and had been now a considerable time with the Indians, and up with them almost as far as Albany, to see King Philip, as he told me, and was now very lately come into these parts. Hearing, I say, that I was in this Indian town, he obtained leave to come and see me. He told me he himself was wounded in the leg at

Here Mary Rowlandson is depicted with her sick child and an Indian guard.

Capt. Beers' fight, and was not able some time to go but as they carried him, and that he took oak leaves and laid to his wound, and by the blessing of God he was able to travel again. Then took I oak leaves and laid to my side, and with the blessing of God it cured me also; yet before the cure was wrought, I may say as it is in Psalms 38:5, 6, "My wounds stink and are corrupt. I am troubled; I am bowed down greatly; I go mourning all the day long." I sat much alone with my poor wounded child in my lap. . . .

Thus nine days I sat upon my knees, with my babe in my lap, till my flesh was raw again. My child being even ready to depart this sorrowful world, they bid me carry it out to another wigwam. . . . About two hours in the night, my sweet babe like a lamb departed this life, on February 18, 1676, it being about six years and five months old. . . . In the morning when they understood that my child was dead, they sent me home to my master's wigwam. By my master in this writing must be understood Quannopin, who was a sagamore, and married King Philip's wife's sister; not that he first took me, but I was sold to him by a Narragansett Indian, who took me when I first came out of the garrison.

I went to take my dead child in my arms to carry it with me, but they bid me let it alone. . . .

Later, the Indians showed Mrs. Rowlandson the hillside grave where they had buried her child.

There I left that child in the wilderness, and must commit it and myself also in this wilderness condition to Him who is above all. God having taken away this dear child, I went to see my daughter Mary, who was at the same Indian town, at a wigwam not very far off, though we had little liberty or opportunity to see one another; she was about ten years old, and taken from the door at first by a praying Indian, and afterwards sold for a gun. When I came in sight, she would fall a-weeping, at which they were provoked, and would not let me come near her, but bid me be gone; which was a heart-cutting word to me. I had one child dead, another in the wilderness, I knew not where, the third they would not let me come near to. . . .

I could not sit still in this condition, but kept walking from one place to another. . . . As I was going up and down, mourning and lamenting my condition, my son [Joseph] came to me and asked me how I did. I had not seen him before since the destruction of the town; and I knew not where he was till I was informed by himself that he was among a smaller parcel of Indians whose place was about six miles off. With tears in his eyes he asked me whether his sister Sarah was dead, and told me he had seen his sister Mary, and prayed me that I would not be troubled in reference to himself. The occasion of his coming to see me was this: there was, as I said, about six miles from us, a small plantation of Indians, where it seems he had been during his captivity, and at this time there were some forces of the Indians gathered out of our company and some also from them, amongst whom was my son's master, to go to assault and burn Medfield. In this time of his master's absence his dame brought him to see me. . . .

The next day the Indians returned from Medfield . . . but before they came to us, oh, the outrageous roaring and whooping that there was! They began their din about a mile before they came to us. By their noise and whooping they signified how many they had destroyed; which was at that time twenty-three. . . . One of the Indians that came from the Medfield fight, and had brought some plunder, came to me and asked me if I would have a Bible; he had got one in his basket. I was glad of it, and asked him if he thought the Indians would let me read. He answered yes. So I took the Bible. . . .

Now the Indians began to talk of removing from this place, some one way and some another. There were now besides myself nine English captives in this place, all of them children except one woman. I got an opportunity to go and take my leave of them, they being to go one way and I another. . . .

Here I parted with my daughter Mary, whom I never saw again till I saw her in Dorchester, returned from captivity, and from four little cousins and neighbors, some of which I never saw afterward; the Lord only knows the end of them. . . .

But to turn to my own journey. We traveled about a half a day or a little more, and came to a desolate place in the wilderness, where there were no wigwams or inhabitants before. We came about the middle of the afternoon to this place, cold, wet, and snowy, and hungry, and weary, and no refreshing for man, but the cold ground to sit on, and our poor Indian cheer.

Heart-aching thoughts here I had about my poor children, who were scattered up and down among the wild beasts of the forest. My head was light and dizzy, either through hunger or bad lodging, or trouble, or all together, my knees feeble, my body raw by sitting double night and day, that I cannot express to man the affliction that lay upon my spirit, but the Lord helped me at that time to express it to Himself. I opened my Bible to read and the Lord brought that precious scripture to me, Jeremiah 31:16—"Thus saith the Lord, refrain thy voice from weeping and thine eyes from tears, for thy work shall be rewarded, and they shall come again from the land of the enemy." This was a sweet cordial to me when I was ready to faint. Many and many a time have I sat down and wept sweetly over this scripture. At this place we continued about four days.

The occasion, as I thought, of their removing at this time was the English army's being near and following them; for they went as if they had gone for their lives for some considerable way; and then they made a stop, and chose out some of their stoutest men, and sent them back to hold the English army in play whilst the rest escaped. . . . Some carried their old, decrepit mothers, some carried one, and some another. Four of them carried a great Indian upon a bier; but going through a thick wood with him, they were hindered and could make no haste; whereupon they took him upon their backs and carried him one at a time till we came to Bacquag River. Upon Friday, a little after noon, we came to this river. . . . They quickly fell to cutting dry trees, to make rafts to carry them over the river, and soon my turn came to go over. . . . On the Saturday they boiled an old horse's leg which they had got, and so we drank of the broth, as soon as they thought it was ready, and when it was almost all gone they filled it up again.

The first week of my being among them, I hardly eat anything; the second week I found my stomach grow very faint for want of something, and yet it was very hard to get down their filthy trash; but the third week, though I could think how formerly my stomach would turn against this or that, and I could starve and die before I could eat such things, yet they were pleasant and savory to my taste. . . .

And here I cannot but take notice of the strange providence of God in preserving the heathen. They were many hundreds, old and young, some sick and some lame; many had papooses on their backs; the greatest number at this time with us were squaws; and yet they traveled with all they had, bag and baggage, and they got over the river aforesaid; and on Monday they set their wigwams afire and away they went. On that very day came the English army after them to this river, and saw the smoke of their wigwams, and yet this river put a stop to them. . . .

We came that day to a great swamp, by the side of which we took up our lodging that night. When we came to the brow of the hill that looked toward the swamp, I thought we had come to a great Indian town, though there were none but our own company. The Indians were as thick as the trees; it seemed as if there had been a thousand hatchets going at once. If one looked before one there was nothing but Indians, and behind one nothing but Indians; and so on either hand; and I myself in the midst, and no Christian soul near me, and yet how hath the Lord preserved me in safety. . . .

After a restless and hungry night there, we had a wearisome time of it the next day. The swamp by which we lay was as it were a deep dungeon, and an exceeding high and steep hill before it. Before I got to the top of the hill, I thought my heart and legs and all would have broken and failed me. . . .

That day, a little after noon, we came to Squaheag [Northfield], where the Indians quickly spread themselves over the deserted English fields, gleaning what they could find. Some picked up ears of wheat that were crickled down, some found ears of Indian corn, some found groundnuts, and others sheaves of wheat that were frozen together in the shock, and went to threshing of them out. Myself got two ears of Indian corn, and whilst I did but turn my back, one of them was stole from me, which much troubled me. There came an Indian to them at that time with a basket of horse liver. I asked him to give me a piece. "What," says he, "can you eat horse liver?" I told him I would try, if he would give me a piece, which he did; and I laid it on the coals to roast; but before it was half ready, they got half of it away from me; so that I was forced to take the rest and eat it as it was, with the blood about my mouth, and yet a savory bit it was to me; for to the hungry soul every bitter thing is sweet.

The next morning the company started to cross the Connecticut River to meet with King Philip. Some English scouts in the neighborhood scattered the Indians, however. During this interlude, Mrs. Rowlandson met her son unexpectedly and they were able to have a brief chat. Her band of Indians traveled on until nightfall, and in the morning succeeded in reaching the other side of the river.

When I was in the canoe, I could not but be amazed at the numerous crew of pagans that were on the bank on the other side. When I came ashore, they gathered all about me; I was sitting alone in the midst. I observed they asked one another questions, and laughed, and rejoiced over their gains and victories. Then my heart began to fail, and I fell a-weeping, which was the first time, to my remembrance, that I wept before them. . . . There one of them asked me why I wept. I could hardly tell what to say; yet I answered, they would kill me. "No," said he, "none will hurt you." Then came one of them and gave me two spoonfuls of meal, to comfort me, and another gave me half a pint of peas, which was worth more than many bushels at

another time. Then I went to see King Philip. He bade me
come in and sit down, and asked me whether I would smoke it
—a usual compliment nowadays among the saints and sinners;
but this no way suited me; for though I had formerly used
tobacco, yet I had left it ever since I was first taken. . . .

Now the Indians gathered their forces to go against Northampton. Overnight one went about yelling and hooting to
give notice of the design. Whereupon they went to boiling of
groundnuts and parching corn, as many as had it, for their provision; and in the morning away they went. During my abode in
this place, Philip spake to me to make a shirt for his boy, which
I did; for which he gave me a shilling. I offered the money to
my mistress, but she bid me keep it, and with it I bought a
piece of horseflesh. Afterward he [Philip] asked me to make a
cap for his boy, for which he invited me to dinner. I went, and
he gave me a pancake about as big as two fingers; it was made
of parched wheat, beaten and fried in bear's grease, but I
thought I never tasted pleasanter meat in my life.

There was a squaw who spake to me to make a shirt for her
Sannup [husband]; for which she gave me a piece of beef.
Another asked me to knit a pair of stockings, for which she gave
me a quart of peas. I boiled my peas and beef together, and
invited my master and mistress to dinner; but the proud gossip,
because I served them both in one dish, would eat nothing,
except one bit that he gave her upon the point of his knife. . . .

The Indians returning from Northampton brought with
them some horses and sheep and other things which they had
taken. I desired them that they would carry me to Albany upon
one of those horses, and sell me for [gun] powder; for so they
had sometimes discoursed. I was utterly helpless of getting
home on foot, the way that I came. I could hardly bear to think
of the many weary steps I had taken to this place.

But instead of either going to Albany or homeward, we
must go five miles up the river, and then go over it. Here we
abode a while. Here lived a sorry Indian, who spake to me to
make him a shirt; when I had done it he would pay me nothing
for it. But he living by the riverside, where I often went to fetch
water, I would often be putting him in mind, and calling for my
pay. At last he told me if I would make another shirt for a
papoose not yet born, he would give me a knife, which he did

when I had done it. I carried the knife in, and my master asked me to give it to him, and I was not a little glad that I had anything that they would accept of and be pleased with. When we were at this place, my master's maid came home; she had been gone three weeks into the Narragansett country to fetch corn, where they had stored up some in the ground. She brought home about a peck and a half of corn. . . .

My son being now about a mile from me, I asked liberty to go and see him. They bid me go, and away I went; but quickly lost myself, traveling over hills and through swamps, and could not find the way to him. And I cannot but admire at the wonderful power and goodness of God to me, in that though I was gone from home and met all sorts of Indians, and those I had no knowledge of, and there being no Christian soul near me, yet not one of them offered the least imaginable miscarriage to me. I turned homeward again, and met with my master, and he showed me the way to my son.

When Mrs. Rowlandson returned from seeing her son, she was hungry, but there was no food in her master's home. She went into another wigwam, where she found an Indian woman who gave her a piece of bear meat. The next day, the same woman gave her some groundnuts. One cold night, when Mrs. Rowlandson could find no room to sit before the fire in her master's wigwam, people in another home made her welcome and invited her to come again. She mentions many such kindnesses from Indians who were total strangers to her.

After a while, the group Mrs. Rowlandson was with moved five or six miles downriver, where they stayed for about two weeks. During this time the Indians raided Hadley and brought back with them one captive, Thomas Reed. Mrs. Rowlandson had an opportunity to talk with him and ask after her husband. Reed reported him to be well, but saddened by the loss of his wife and children.

At this place there was also a captive English youth whom Mrs. Rowlandson found lying on the ground, almost dead from exposure to the cold winter weather. She succeeded in getting him to a wigwam, but at some cost to herself, for the rumor started that she and the young man were planning to escape. When her master and mistress heard this, they threatened to kill her if she went outside the wigwam again. She was now in a perilous situation, because if she stayed in, she would starve to death, and if she went out she would be "knocked on the head," as she says. Luck remained with her, however. After a day and a half

> . . . came an Indian to me with a pair of stockings which were too big for him, and he would have me ravel them out, and knit them fit for him. I showed myself willing, and bid him ask my mistress if I might go along with him a little way. She said yes, I might; but I was not a little refreshed with that news, that I had my liberty again. Then I went along with him, and he gave me some roasted groundnuts, which did again revive my feeble stomach. . . .

> Then my son came to see me, and I asked his master to let him stay a while with me, that I might comb his head and look over him, for he was almost overcome with lice. He told me when I was done that he was very hungry, but I had nothing to relieve him, but bid him go into the wigwams as he went along, and see if he could get anything among them; which he did, and, it seems, tarried a little too long, for his master was angry with him, and beat him, and then sold him. Then he came running to tell me he had a new master, and that he had given him some groundnuts already. Then I went along with him to his new master, who told me he loved him, and he should not want. So his master carried him away; and I never saw him afterward, till I saw him at Piscataqua, in Portsmouth [after both Mrs. Rowlandson and her son had been released from captivity]. . . .

Previously, Mrs. Rowlandson's hopes of being ransomed had been raised when the Indians started easterly in the direction of Boston. Her mistress finally refused to go any farther and turned back with her servants and most of the other Indians. Mrs. Rowlandson's master continued on his way. After some days, the whole group again began an easterly move.

> Now must we pack up and be gone from this thicket, bending our course towards the Bay towns. . . . As we went along, they killed a deer with a young one in her. They gave me a piece of the fawn, and it was so young and tender that one might eat the bones as well as the flesh, and yet I thought it very good.

When night came on, we sat down. It rained, but they quickly got up a bark wigwam, where I lay dry that night. I looked out in the morning, and many of them had lain in the rain all night, I knew by their reeking. Thus the Lord dealt mercifully with me many times, and I fared better than many of them. In the morning they took the blood of the deer and put it into the paunch, and so boiled it. I could eat nothing of that, though they eat it sweetly. And yet they were so nice in other things that when I had fetched water and had put the dish I dipped the water with into the kettle of water which I brought, they would say they would knock me down, for they said it was a sluttish trick.

We went on our travel. I having got a handful of ground-nuts for my support that day, they gave me my load and I went on cheerfully, with the thoughts of going homeward, having my burden more upon my back than my spirit. We came to Bacquag River again that day, near which we abode a few days. Sometimes one of them would give me a pipe, another a little tobacco, another a little salt, which I would change for victuals. I cannot but think what a wolfish appetite persons have in a starving condition. . . .

When the Indians once again started moving eastward,

. . . quickly there came up to us an Indian who informed them that I must go to Wachuset to my master, for there was a letter come from the [colonists'] council to the sagamores about redeeming the captives, and that there would be another in fourteen days, and that I must be there ready. My heart was so heavy before that I could scarce speak or go in the path, and yet now so light that I could run. My strength seemed to come again and to recruit my feeble knees and aching heart; yet it pleased them to go but one mile that night, and there we stayed two days. . . .

When the Indians started out again, Mrs. Rowlandson was full of optimism.

A comfortable remove it was to me, because of my hopes. They gave me my pack and along we went cheerfully. But quickly my will proved more than my strength; having little or no refreshment, my strength failed, and my spirits were almost gone. . . .

At night we came to an Indian town, and the Indians sat down by a wigwam discoursing, but I was almost spent and could scarce speak. I laid down my load and went into the wigwam, and there sat an Indian boiling of horse feet, they being wont to eat the flesh first, and when the feet were old and dried, and they had nothing else, they would cut off the feet and use them. I asked him to give me a little of his broth, or water they were boiling it in. He took a dish and gave me one spoonful of samp, and bid me take as much of the broth as I would. Then I put some of the hot water to the samp, and drank it up, and my spirits came again.

There were two more days of traveling.

At last, after many weary steps, I saw Wachuset hills, but many miles off. Then we came to a great swamp, through which we traveled up to our knees in mud and water, which was heavy going to one tired before. Being almost spent, I thought I should have sunk down at last and never got out. . . . Going along, having indeed my life but little spirit, Philip, who was in the company, came up and took me by the hand, and said, "Two weeks more and you shall be mistress again." I asked him if he spoke true. He said, "Yes, and quickly you shall come to your master again"; who had been gone from us three weeks. After many weary steps we came to Wachuset, where he [the chief who was Mrs. Rowlandson's master] was, and glad was I to see him. He asked me when I washed me. I told him not this month. Then he fetched me some water himself, and bid me wash, and gave me a glass to see how I looked, and bid his squaw give me something to eat. So she gave me a mess of beans and meat, and a little groundnut cake. I was wonderfully revived with this favor showed me. . . .

My master had three squaws, living sometimes with one and sometimes with another: Onux, this old squaw at whose wigwam I was, and with whom my master had been these three weeks. Another was Wettimore, with whom I had lived and served all this while. A severe and proud dame she was, bestowing every day in dressing herself near as much time as any of the gentry of the land; powdering her hair and painting her face, going with her necklaces, with jewels in her ears, and bracelets upon her hands. When she had dressed herself, her work was to make girdles of wampum and beads. The third squaw was a younger one, by whom he had two papooses. By that time I was refreshed by the old squaw, Wettimore's maid came to call me home, at which I fell a-weeping. Then the old squaw told me, to encourage me, that when I wanted victuals I should come to her, and that I should be in her wigwam. Then I went with the maid, and quickly I came back and lodged there. The squaw laid a mat under me and a good rug over me; the first time that I had any such kindness showed me. I understood that Wettimore thought that if she should let me go and serve with the old squaw she would be in danger to lose not only my service, but the redemption pay also. . . .

Then came Tom and Peter [Indian messengers] with the second letter from the council about the captives. . . . The sagamores . . . called me to them to inquire how much my husband would give to redeem me. . . . Now knowing that all that we had was destroyed by the Indians, I was in a great strait. I thought if I should speak of but a little, it would be slighted and hinder the matter; if of a great sum, I knew not where it could be procured; yet at a venture I said twenty pounds, yet desired them to take less; but they would not hear of that, but sent the message to Boston that for twenty pounds I should be redeemed.

At length, John Hoar, a colonist, came with a third letter from the council. The sum for the ransom had been raised by Boston friends. After a good deal of conferring among the Indians, Mrs. Rowlandson, accompanied by John Hoar and the Indian messengers, was allowed to go to her husband in Boston.

At first, they [the Indians] were all against it, except my husband would come for me; but afterward they assented to it, and seeming to rejoice in it; some asking me to send them some bread, others some tobacco, others shaking me by the hand, offering me a hood and a scarf to ride in; not one moving hand or tongue against it. . . .

So I took my leave of them, and in coming along, my heart melted into tears more than all the while I was with them, and I was almost swallowed up with the thoughts that ever I should go home again.

Some other members of the family were still missing. The

The release of captives prompted joy and tears. For some, however, there were mixed feelings and divided loyalties.

week after Mrs. Rowlandson's return her sister was released, but the whereabouts of the Rowlandson children remained unknown. Their mother spent many anxious hours worrying over their fate in the wilderness. At last, one happy day, word came that Joseph and one of his cousins had been returned in Portsmouth, New Hampshire. The next day, news arrived that ten-year-old Mary had been brought into Providence, Rhode Island, by an Indian woman who had helped her escape. Friends brought the girl to her parents in Dorchester, and the Rowlandsons went to Portsmouth for a jubilant reunion with their son.

Now that the family was together once again, the congregation of the South Church in Boston hired a house for them. Here they stayed for about nine months. They had no possessions, but they had good friends, as Mrs. Rowlandson realized.

I thought it somewhat strange to set up housekeeping with bare walls, but as Solomon says, "Money answers all things," and this we had through the benevolence of friends, some in this town, some in that, and some from England, that in a little time we might look and see the house furnished with love.

Mrs. Rowlandson had been through a dreadful ordeal, but staunch Puritan that she was, she looked at the positive side of her experience. She ended her account with the following words:

Yet I see when God calls persons to never so many difficulties, yet he is able to carry them through, and make them say they have been gainers thereby; and I hope I can say, in some measure, as David, "It is good for me that I have been afflicted." The Lord hath showed me the vanity of these outward things, that they are vanities of vanities and vexation of spirit; that they are but a shadow, a blast, a bubble, and things of no continuance. If trouble from smaller matter begin to rise in me, I have something at hand to check myself with, and say, "Why am I troubled?" It was but the other day that if I had the world I would have given it for my freedom, or to have been a servant to a Christian. I have learned to look beyond present and smaller troubles, and to be quieted under them; as Moses said (Exodus 14:13), "Stand still and see the salvation of the Lord."

JAMES SMITH

James Smith was captured in 1755, at the beginning of the French and Indian War.

The French and the British had long been rivals in North America, where the French held territory in New France, now Canada, and the British had colonies on a long strip of coast east of the Appalachian Mountains. When both countries attempted to occupy the rich Ohio Valley, trouble began.

The French wished to build a chain of forts and trading posts that would join their settlements on the lower Mississippi River with their territory in New France. The British saw that any such development would box them into an area along the coast. They realized that the Ohio Valley was a promising place for settlement by their colonists.

When the French began to build their forts, the British sent them a letter, warning them off. The warning was ineffective. In 1755, the British decided to attack some of the French strongholds. General Edward Braddock, British commander in chief, led the expedition to capture Fort Duquesne, situated where Pittsburgh, Pennsylvania, now stands. Braddock suffered a devas-

These men are reenacting the trading relationship between the French and the Indians. Often gifts were given to the Indians to ensure their goodwill in the coming fight with the British.

tating defeat in a wilderness battle that was the beginning of the French and Indian War.

James Smith gives us a helpless bystander's view of that defeat as he witnessed it while a captive of the French and their Indian allies at Fort Duquesne. What he saw sickened him against the Indians for months, but their good will toward him and their concern and pride in seeing him become a worthy member of the tribe eventually overcame his animosity. His story is a warm and winning one. He starts it in this way.

In May, 1755, the province of Pennsylvania agreed to send out

three hundred men, in order to cut a wagon road from Fort
Loudon to join Braddock's road near the Turkey Foot, or three
forks of Yohogania. My brother-in-law, William Smith, Esq. of
Conococheague was appointed commissioner, to have the over-
sight of these roadcutters.

Though I was at that time only eighteen years of age, I had
fallen violently in love with a young lady, whom I apprehended
was possessed of a large share of both beauty and virtue; but
being born between Venus and Mars, I concluded I must also
leave my dear fair one and go out with this company of roadcutters, to see the event of this campaign; but still expecting that
some time in the course of this summer I should again return to
the arms of my beloved.

We went on with the road without interruption until near
the Allegheny Mountain, when I was sent back in order to
hurry up some provision wagons that were on the way after us. I
proceeded down the road as far as the crossings of Juniata,
where, finding the wagons were coming on as fast as possible, I
returned up the road again towards the Allegheny Mountain, in
company with one Arnold Vigoras. About four or five miles
above Bedford, three Indians had made a blind of bushes, stuck
in the ground as though they grew naturally, where they concealed themselves, about fifteen yards from the road. When we
came opposite to them, they fired upon us at this short distance
and killed my fellow traveler, yet their bullets did not touch me;
but my horse making a violent start, threw me, and the Indians
immediately ran up and took me prisoner. The one that laid
hold on me was a Canasatauga, the other two were Delawares.
One of them could speak English, and asked me if there were
any more white men coming after. I told them not any near
that I knew of. Two of these Indians stood by me, whilst the
other scalped my comrade; they then set off and ran at a smart
rate through the woods for about fifteen miles, and that night
we slept on the Allegheny Mountain without fire.

The next morning they divided the last of their provision
which they had brought from Fort Duquesne, and gave me an
equal share, which was about two or three ounces of moldy bis-
cuit; this and a young groundhog about as large as a rabbit,
roasted and also equally divided, was all the provision we had
until we came to the Loyal Hannan, which was about fifty

miles; and a great part of the way we came through exceeding rocky laurel thickets, without any path. When we came to the west side of Laurel Hill, they gave a scalp halloo, as usual, which is a long yell or halloo for every scalp or prisoner they have in possession; the last of these scalp halloos were followed with quick and sudden shrill shouts of joy and triumph. On their performing this, we were answered by the firing of a number of guns on the Loyal Hannan, one after another, quicker than one could count, by another party of Indians, who were encamped near where Ligoneer now stands. As we advanced near this party they increased with repeated shouts of joy and triumph; but I did not share with them in their excessive mirth. When we came to this camp, we found they had plenty of turkeys and other meat there; and though I never before eat venison without bread or salt, yet as I was hungry it relished very well. There we lay that night, and the next morning the whole of us marched on our way for Fort Duquesne. The night after, we joined another camp of Indians, with nearly the same ceremony, attended with great noise, and apparent joy among all except one. The next morning we continued our march, and in the afternoon we came in full view of the fort, which stood on the point, near where Fort Pitt now stands. We then made a halt on the bank of the Allegheny and repeated the scalp halloo, which was answered by the firing of all the firelocks in the hands of both Indians and French who were in and about the fort, in the aforesaid manner, and also the great guns, which were followed by the continued shouts and yells of the different savage tribes who were then collected there.

As I was at this time unacquainted with this mode of firing and yelling of the savages, I concluded that there were thousands of Indians there ready to receive General Braddock; but what added to my surprise, I saw numbers running towards me, stripped naked, excepting breechclouts, and painted in the most hideous manner, of various colors, though the principal color was vermilion, or a bright red; yet there was annexed to this black, brown, blue, etc. As they approached they formed themselves into two long ranks, about two or three rods apart. I was told by an Indian that could speak English that I must run betwixt these ranks, and that they would flog me all the way as I ran; and if I ran quick, it would be so much the better as they would quit when I got to the end of the ranks. There appeared to be a general rejoicing around me, yet I could find nothing like joy in my breast; but I started to the race with all the resolution and vigor I was capable of exerting, and found that it was as I had been told, for I was flogged the whole way. When I had got near the end of the lines, I was struck with something that appeared to me to be a stick or the handle of a tomahawk, which caused me to fall to the ground. On my recovering my senses, I endeavored to renew my race; but as I arose someone cast sand in my eyes, which blinded me so that I could not see where to run. They continued beating me most intolerably, until I was at length insensible; but before I lost my senses, I remember my wishing them to strike the fatal blow, for I thought they intended killing me, but apprehended they were too long about it.

When Smith regained consciousness he was inside the fort, and a French doctor was washing his wounds. After the Indians had questioned him about the three hundred Pennsylvanians who were building the road to join Braddock, he was sent to the hospital. There he received good care and recovered quickly.

Some time after I was there, I was visited by the Delaware Indian already mentioned, who was at the taking of me and could speak some English. Though he spoke but bad English, yet I found him to be a man of considerable understanding. I asked him if I had done anything that had offended the Indians which caused them to treat me so unmercifully. He said no; it was only an old custom the Indians had, and it was like how do you do; after that, he said, I would be well used. I asked him if I should be admitted to remain with the French. He said no; and told me that, as soon as I recovered, I must not only go with the Indians, but must be made an Indian myself. I asked him what news from Braddock's army. He said the Indians spied them every day, and he showed me, by making marks on the ground with a stick, that Braddock's army was advancing in very close order, and that the Indians would surround them, take trees, and (as he expressed it) *shoot um down all one pigeon.*

Shortly after this, on July 9, 1755, there was a great stir in the fort. Investigating, Smith found that the French and Indians

were marching out against Braddock. He estimated that about
four hundred men made up the company and he marveled that
so small a party could hope to overcome the British. In the
afternoon he heard shouts of joy. Upon inquiring the cause, he
was told that a runner had just arrived to say that Braddock
would surely be defeated; the Indians and French had surrounded
his troops and were firing on them. The English were "falling
in heaps" and if they did not reach the river gap and make their
escape, not a man would be left alive by nightfall.

> Some time after this I heard a number of scalp halloos and saw
> a company of Indians and French coming in. I observed they
> had a great many bloody scalps, grenadiers' caps, British can-
> teens, bayonets, etc., with them. They brought the news that
> Braddock was defeated. After that another company came in,
> which appeared to be about one hundred, and chiefly Indians,
> and it seemed to me that almost every one of this company was
> carrying scalps; after this came another company with a number
> of wagon horses, and also a great many scalps.

About a dozen British prisoners were brought in alive. Smith
watched in horror as they were tied to stakes to be burned, then
fled to his sleeping quarters.

> When I came into my lodgings I saw Russel's *Seven Sermons*,
> which they had brought from the field of battle, which a
> Frenchman made a present to me. From the best information I
> could receive, there were only seven Indians and four French
> killed in this battle, and five hundred British lay dead in the
> field, besides what were killed in the river on their retreat.
>   The morning after the battle I saw Braddock's artillery
> brought into the fort; the same day I also saw several Indians in
> British officers' dress, with sash, half moon, laced hats, etc.,
> which the British then wore.

A few days after this the Indians took Smith to a village
about forty miles above Fort Duquesne. Three weeks later he
was transferred to another village called Tullihas, which was
inhabited by members of the Delaware, Caughnewaga, and
Mohican tribes.

> The day after my arrival at the aforesaid town, a number of
> Indians collected about me, and one of them began to pull the

Burning the prisoners

hair out of my head. He had some ashes on a piece of bark, in which he frequently dipped his fingers, in order to take the firmer hold, and so he went on, as if he had been plucking a turkey, until he had all the hair clean out of my head, except a small spot about three or four inches square on my crown; this they cut off with a pair of scissors, excepting three locks, which they dressed up in their own mode. Two of these they wrapped round with a narrow beaded garter made by themselves for that purpose, and the other they plaited at full length, and then stuck it full of silver brooches. After this they bored my nose and ears, and fixed me off with earrings and nose jewels; then they ordered me to strip off my clothes and put on a breechclout, which I did; they then painted my head, face, and body in various colors. They put a large belt of wampum on my neck, and silver bands on my hands and right arm; and so an old chief led me out in the street and gave the alarm halloo, *coo-wigh*, several times repeated quick; and on this, all that were in the town came running and stood round the old chief, who held me by the hand in the midst. As I at that time knew nothing of their mode of adoption and had seen them put to death all they had taken, and I never could find that they saved a man alive at Braddock's defeat, I made no doubt but they were about putting me to death in some cruel manner.

After the old chief had made a long speech to the assembled crowd, he handed Smith over to three young Indian women. They led him to the river and guided him out until the water was about waist-high. There they made signs to him that he was to plunge in. Thinking they were trying to drown him, Smith refused to obey. The three women seized him and tried to duck him. He resisted, to the great amusement of the Indians on the riverbank. Finally one of the women made him understand that they would not hurt him. With that reassurance he allowed himself to be immersed in the water, where he was washed and rubbed by the three women.

> These young women then led me up to the council house, where some of the tribe were ready with new clothes for me. They gave me a new ruffled shirt, which I put on, also a pair of leggins done off with ribbons and beads, likewise a pair of moccasins, and garters dressed with beads, porcupine quills, and red hair—also a tinsel-laced cappo [cloak]. They again painted my head and face with various colors, and tied a bunch of red feathers to one of those locks they had left on the crown of my head, which stood up five or six inches. They seated me on a bearskin and gave me a pipe, tomahawk, and polecat-skin pouch, which had been skinned pocket fashion and contained tobacco, killegenico, or dry sumach leaves, which they mix with their tobacco; also spunk, flint, and steel. When I was thus seated, the Indians came in dressed and painted in their grandest manner. As they came in they took their seats, and for a considerable time there was a profound silence—everyone was smoking; but not a word was spoken among them. At length

one of the chiefs made a speech, which was delivered to me by an interpreter, and was as followeth: "My son, you are now flesh of our flesh, and bone of our bone. By the ceremony which was performed this day every drop of white blood was washed out of your veins; you are taken into the Caughnewaga nation and initiated into a warlike tribe; you are adopted into a great family, and now received with great seriousness and solemnity in the room and place of a great man. After what has passed this day, you are now one of us by an old strong law and custom. My son, you have now nothing to fear—we are now under the same obligations to love, support, and defend you that we are to love and to defend one another; therefore, you are to consider yourself as one of our people."

At this time I did not believe this fine speech, especially that of the white blood being washed out of me; but since that time I have found that there was much sincerity in said speech; for, from that day, I never knew them to make any distinction between me and themselves in any respect whatever until I left them. If they had plenty of clothing, I had plenty; if we were scarce, we all shared one fate.

After the ceremony, Smith was introduced to his new kin, and in the evening he attended a feast and dance. The next day some of the men left on a war raid against the Virginia frontier. The remaining men instructed Smith in hunting and gave him a gun.

Some time after this, I was told to take the dogs with me and go down the creek; perhaps I might kill a turkey. It being in the afternoon, I was also told not to go far from the creek, and to come up the creek again to the camp, and to take care not to get lost. When I had gone some distance down the creek, I came upon fresh buffalo tracks, and as I had a number of dogs with me to stop the buffalo, I concluded I would follow after and kill one; and as the grass and weeds were rank, I could readily follow the track. A little before sundown I despaired of coming up with them. I was then thinking how I might get to camp before night. I concluded, as the buffalo had made several turns, if I took the track back to the creek it would be dark before I could get to camp; therefore I thought I would take a near way through the hills and strike the creek a little below the

camp; but as it was cloudy weather and I a very young woods-
man, I could find neither creek nor camp. When night came on
I fired my gun several times and hallooed, but could have no
answer. The next morning early the Indians were out after me,
and as I had with me ten or a dozen dogs, and the grass and
weeds rank, they could readily follow my track. When they
came up with me, they appeared to be in very good humor. I
asked Solomon [one of the Indians] if he thought I was running away; he said, "No, no, you too much crooked." On my
return to camp they took my gun from me, and for this rash
step I was reduced to a bow and arrows for nearly two years.

When the war party returned, they had an English Bible
among their loot. This book was given to Smith.

I remained in this town until some time in October when my
adopted brother, called Tontileaugo, who had married a Wyandot squaw, took me with him to Lake Erie. . . .

On this route we had no horses with us, and when we
started from the town all the pack I carried was a pouch containing my books, a little dried venison, and my blanket. I had
then no gun, but Tontileaugo, who was a first-rate hunter, carried a rifle gun, and every day killed deer, raccoons, or bears.
We left the meat, excepting a little for present use, and carried
the skins with us until we encamped, and then stretched them
with elm bark, in a frame made with poles stuck in the ground,
and tied together with lynn or elm bark; and when the skins
were dried by the fire, we packed them up and carried them
with us the next day.

As Tontileaugo could not speak English, I had to make use
of all the Caughnewaga I had learned, even to talk very imperfectly with him; but I found I learned to talk Indian faster this
way than when I had those with me who could speak English.

The two men proceeded down the Canesadooharie River
until they reached Lake Erie.

Some time in the afternoon we came to a large camp of Wyan-
dots, at the mouth of Canesadooharie, where Tontileaugo's wife
was. Here we were kindly received. . . .

We continued our camp at the mouth of Canesadooharie
for some time, where we killed some deer and a great many rac-

coons; the raccoons here were remarkably large and fat. At length we all embarked in a large birchbark canoe. This vessel was about four feet wide and three feet deep, and about five and thirty feet long; and though it could carry a heavy burden, it was so artfully and curiously constructed that four men could carry it several miles, or from one landing place to another, or from the waters of the lake to the waters of the Ohio. We proceeded up Canesadooharie a few miles, and went on shore to hunt; but to my great surprise they carried the vessel we all came in up the bank, and inverted it or turned the bottom up, and converted it to a dwelling house, and kindled a fire before us to warm ourselves by and cook. With our baggage and ourselves in this house we were very much crowded, yet our little house turned off the rain very well. . . .

While we remained here I left my pouch with my books in camp, wrapped up in my blanket, and went out to hunt chestnuts. On my return to camp my books were missing. I inquired after them, and asked the Indians if they knew where they were; they told me that they supposed the puppies had carried them off. I did not believe them, but thought they were displeased at my poring over my books, and concluded that they had destroyed them, or put them out of my way.

After some weeks of hunting along the river the Indians buried their canoe in the ground, to preserve it from the winter weather. After they had packed their goods, they headed east to a large creek where they built a snug winter cabin of timber and bark.

It was some time in December when we finished this winter cabin; but when we had got into this comparatively fine lodging, another difficulty arose; we had nothing to eat. While I was traveling with Tontileaugo, as was before mentioned, and had plenty of fat venison, bear's meat, and raccoons, I then thought it was hard living without bread and salt; but now I began to conclude that if I had anything that would banish pinching hunger and keep soul and body together, I would be content.

While the hunters were all out, exerting themselves to the utmost of their ability, the squaws and boys (in which class I was) were scattered out in the bottoms, hunting red haws, black haws, and hickory nuts. As it was too late in the year, we did not succeed in gathering haws; but we had tolerable success in scratching up hickory nuts from under a light snow, which we carried with us lest the hunters should not succeed. After our return the hunters came in, who had killed only two small turkeys, which were but little among eight hunters and thirteen squaws, boys, and children; but they were divided with the greatest equity and justice—everyone got their equal share.

The next day the hunters turned out again, and killed one deer and three bears.

One of the bears was very large and remarkably fat. The hunters carried in meat sufficient to give us all a hearty supper and breakfast.

The squaws and all that could carry turned out to bring in meat—everyone had their share assigned them, and my load was among the least; yet, not being accustomed to carrying in this way, I got exceeding weary and told them my load was too heavy, I must leave part of it and come for it again. They made a halt and only laughed at me, and took part of my load and added it to a young squaw's, who had as much before as I carried.

This kind of reproof had a greater tendency to excite me to exert myself in carrying without complaining than if they had whipped me for laziness. After this the hunters held a council and concluded that they must have horses to carry their loads; and that they would go to war even in this inclement season, in order to bring in horses.

Four of the men were chosen to go on the war expedition, while Tontileaugo and three others, because they were the best hunters, remained at home to provide food for the camp. After the warriors left, times were hard, as hunting conditions were unfavorable. At length, Tontileaugo took young Smith with him on a trip to look for holes where bears might be hibernating.

The next morning early we proceeded on and when we found a tree scratched by the bears climbing up, and the hole in the tree sufficiently large for the reception of the bear, we then felled a sapling or small tree against or near the hole; and it was my business to climb up and drive out the bear while Tontileaugo stood ready with his gun and bow. We went on in this manner until evening, without success. At length we found a large elm scratched, and a hole in it about forty feet up; but no tree nigh suitable to lodge against the hole. Tontileaugo got a long pole and some dry rotten wood, which he tied in bunches, with bark; and as there was a tree that grew near the elm and extended up near the hole, but leaned the wrong way, so that we could not lodge it to advantage, to remedy this inconvenience he climbed up this tree and carried with him his rotten wood, fire, and pole. The rotten wood he tied to his belt, and to one end of the pole he tied a hook and a piece of rotten wood, which he set fire to, as it would retain fire almost like spunk, and reached this hook from limb to limb as he went up. When he got up with his pole he put dry wood on fire into the hole; after he put in the fire he heard the bear snuff, and he came speedily down, took his gun in his hand, and waited until the bear would come out; but it was some time before it appeared, and when it did appear he attempted taking sight with his rifle; but it being then too dark to see the sights, he set it down by a tree, and instantly bent his bow, took hold of an arrow, and shot the bear a little behind the shoulder. I was preparing also to shoot an arrow, but he called me to stop, there was no occasion; and with that the bear fell to the ground.

Being very hungry, we kindled a fire, opened the bear, took out the liver, and wrapped some of the caul fat round, and put it on a wooden spit, which we stuck in the ground by the fire to roast; then we skinned the bear, got on our kettle, and had both roast and boiled, and also sauce to our meat, which appeared to me to be delicate fare.

Smith and Tontileaugo stayed in this vicinity for about two weeks; during that time they killed four bears, several turkeys, three deer, and a number of raccoons. When they returned to the winter camp with as much meat as they could carry, there was great joy; the Indians they had left behind were near starvation. After everyone had eaten, all those who were able went out and brought in the remainder of the meat. Several weeks later, the warriors returned with two scalps and six horses that they had taken from pioneers on the Pennsylvania frontier. With the horses, the hunters could travel farther from camp and could bring in meat more easily; from this time on, there were usually plenty of provisions. In February, the Indians began to make maple sugar.

As some of the elm bark will strip at this season, the squaws,
after finding a tree that would do, cut it down and with a
crooked stick, broad and sharp at the end, took the bark off the
tree, and of this bark made vessels in a curious manner, that
would hold about two gallons each; they made above one
hundred of these kind of vessels. In the [maple] sugar tree they
cut a notch, sloping down, and at the end of the notch stuck in
a tomahawk; in the place where they stuck the tomahawk they
drove a long chip, in order to carry the water [sap] out from
the tree, and under this they set their vessel to receive it. As
sugar trees were plenty and large here, they seldom or never
notched a tree that was not two or three feet over [in
diameter]. They also made bark vessels for carrying the water,
that would hold about four gallons each. They had two brass
kettles that held about fifteen gallons each, and other smaller
kettles in which they boiled the water. But as they could not at
times boil away the water as fast as it was collected, they made
vessels of bark that would hold about one hundred gallons each,
for retaining the water; and though the sugar trees did not run
every day, they had always a sufficient quantity of water to keep
them boiling during the whole sugar season.

The way we commonly used our sugar while encamped was
by putting it in bear's fat until the fat was almost as sweet as
the sugar itself, and in this we dipped our roasted venison. . . .

About the latter end of March we began to prepare for
moving into town in order to plant corn. The squaws were then
frying the last of their bear's fat, and making vessels to hold it;
the vessels were made of deerskins, which were skinned by pulling the skin off the neck without ripping. After they had taken
off the hair, they gathered it in small plaits round the neck and
with a string drew it together like a purse; in the center a pin
was put, below which they tied a string, and while it was wet
they blew it up like a bladder and let it remain in this manner
until it was dry, when it appeared nearly in the shape of a sugar
loaf, but more rounding at the lower end. One of these vessels
would hold about four or five gallons. In these vessels it was
they carried their bear's oil.

When all things were ready, we moved back to the falls of
Canesadooharie. . . .

On our arrival at the falls, as we had brought with us on

horseback about two hundred weight of sugar, a large quantity of bear's oil, skins, etc., the canoe we had buried was not sufficient to carry all; therefore we were obliged to make another one of elm bark. While we lay here, a young Wyandot found my books. On this, they [the Indians] collected together; I was a little way from the camp and saw the collection, but did not know what it meant. They called me by my Indian name, which was Scoouwa, repeatedly. I ran to see what was the matter; they showed me my books and said they were glad they had been found, for they knew I was grieved at the loss of them. As I could then speak some Indian . . . I told them that I thanked them for the kindness they had always shown to me, and also for finding my books. . . . This was the first time that I felt my heart warm towards the Indians. Though they had been exceeding kind to me, I still before detested them, on account of the barbarity I beheld after Braddock's defeat. Neither had I ever before pretended kindness or expressed myself in a friendly manner; but I began now to excuse the Indians on account of their want of information.

When the Indians returned to the Wyandot town, French traders bought their skins and furs in exchange for clothing, paint, tobacco, and other such goods.

All the Indians remained in the town for about six weeks, then the men prepared to go to war against the pioneers on the Virginia frontier. The men and boys marched off, leaving Smith, one very old man, and a lame man of about fifty to provide for the women and children. As they had only one gun, provisions were scarce until the warriors returned, bringing meat with them. At about this same time the green corn was ready to eat. With this food and a supply of venison, the town experienced a period of feasting and idleness.

Some time in October, another adopted brother, older than Tontileaugo, came to pay us a visit at Sunyendeand, and he asked me to take a hunt with him on Cayahaga. As they always used me as a free man, and gave me the liberty of choosing, I told him that I was attached to Tontileaugo, had never seen him before, and therefore asked some time to consider of this. He told me that the party he was going with would not be along, or at the mouth of this little lake, in less than six days, and I could in this time be acquainted with him and judge for myself. I consulted with Tontileaugo on this occasion, and he told me that our old brother Tecaughretanego (which was his name) was a chief, and a better man than he was, and if I went with him I might expect to be well used; but he said I might do as I pleased, and if I stayed he would use me as he had done. I told him that he had acted in every respect as a brother to me; yet I was much pleased with my old brother's conduct and conversation; and as he was going to a part of the country I had never been in, I wished to go with him. He said that he was perfectly willing.

I then went with Tecaughretanego to the mouth of the little lake, where he met with the company he intended going with, which was composed of Caughnewagas and Ottawas.

This company had four birchbark canoes and four reed-mat tents of the kind that the Ottawas used for living quarters. The Indians proceeded along the shores of Lake Erie in their canoes, often using the tent mats as sails. When they came to the mouth of the Cayahaga River they stayed there for several days while they hunted deer. Then they buried their canoes, took all their goods, and marched southeast for about forty miles to the place where they intended to winter. They raised their tents on Beaver Creek, near a little lake. Here Smith had an adventure.

I went out with Tecaughretanego and some others beaver hunting; but we did not succeed, and on our return we saw where several raccoons had passed while the snow was soft. . . . We all made a halt, looking at the raccoon tracks. As they saw a tree with a hole in it, they told me to go and see if they [the raccoons] had gone in thereat; and if they had, to halloo and they would come and take them out. When I went to that tree, I found they had gone past; but I saw another the way they had gone, and proceeded to examine that, and found they had gone up it. I then began to halloo, but could have no answer.

As it began to snow and blow most violently, I returned and proceeded after my company, and for some time could see their tracks; but the old snow being only about three inches deep . . . the present driving snow soon filled up the tracks. As I had only a bow, arrows, and tomahawk with me, and no way to strike fire, I appeared to be in a dismal situation; and as the air was dark with snow, I had little more prospect of steering my course than I would in the night. At length I came to a hollow tree with a hole at one side that I could go in at. I went in, and found that it was a dry place and the hollow about three feet diameter, and high enough for me to stand in. I found that there was also a considerable quantity of soft, dry rotten wood around this hollow; I therefore concluded that I would lodge here, and that I would go to work and stop up the door of my house. I stripped off my blanket (which was all the clothes that I had, excepting a breechclout, leggins, and moccasins), and with my tomahawk fell to chopping at the top of a fallen tree that lay near, and carried wood, and set it up on end against the door, until I had it three or four feet thick all around, excepting a hole I had left to creep in at. I had a block prepared that I could haul after me to stop this hole; and before I went in I put in a number of small sticks that I might more effectually stop it on the inside. When I went in, I took my tomahawk and cut down all the dry rotten wood I could get, and beat it small. With it I made a bed like a goose nest or hog bed, and with the small sticks stopped every hole, until my house was almost dark. I stripped off my moccasins and danced in the center of my bed for about half an hour, in order to warm myself. In this time my feet and whole body were agreeably warmed. The snow, in the meanwhile, had stopped all the holes, so that my house was as dark as a dungeon, though I knew it could not yet be dark out of doors. I then coiled myself in my blanket, lay down in my little round bed, and had a tolerable night's lodging.

Smith awoke in darkness. He could hear the storm still raging, and lay quiet until he felt sure daylight had come. As it was still dark inside the tree, he had some trouble finding the door he had made. When at last he pushed against it, he could not move it. He was terrified that he might be trapped, and sat and thought about his predicament for a while. When he again tried pushing the block of wood that stopped up the opening, it moved about nine inches. He could see that there had been a tremendous fall of snow, which was pressing against the door. With more effort he finally managed to escape from the hollow tree.

I was now in tolerable high spirits, though the snow had fallen above three feet deep, in addition to what was on the ground before; and the only imperfect guide I had in order to steer my course to camp was the trees, as the moss generally grows on the northwest side of them, if they are straight. I proceeded on, wading through the snow, and about twelve o'clock (as it appeared afterwards, from that time to night, for it was yet cloudy) I came upon the creek that our camp was on, about half a mile below the camp; and when I came in sight of the camp I found that there was great joy, by the shouts and yelling of the boys, etc.

The Indians gathered round and welcomed Smith. After they had given him a good meal they asked him to tell his adventure.

I told them the whole of the story, and they never interrupted me, but when I made a stop, the intervals were filled with loud acclamations of joy.

When Smith had finished, Tecaughretanego made a speech, saying that the Indians had been about to go in search of him, although they feared he might have perished in the storm. Tecaughretanego went on to say:

Now we are glad to see you in various respects: we are glad to see you on your own account; and we are glad to see the prospect of your filling the place of a great man, in whose room [place] you were adopted. . . . Your conduct on this occasion hath pleased us; you have given us an evidence of your fortitude, skill, and resolution; and we hope you will always go on to do great actions, as it is only great actions that can make a great man.

About two weeks later, Smith went out to check the beaver traps and was overtaken by darkness. He had no means of making a fire and "danced and hallooed" all night to keep himself from freezing to death. When he came into camp the next morning, the Indians were tolerant of his lapse. They said that in this place, with its intricate pattern of beaver ponds, they had often found themselves in the same predicament. They were pleased with his endurance and, as they now had plenty of beaver skins, they promised to get him a new gun in Detroit in the spring. So, as Smith says, "By lying out two nights here I regained my credit." No longer would he have to rely on a bow and arrow.

In February the company packed up their furs and moved to a place about ten miles away, where the women busied themselves with making maple sugar. After that work was done, the Indians went to Detroit to trade their furs; there Smith received his gun. Summer was spent in growing corn, in idling, and in warring on the frontier. Around the first of November, a number of families started for their winter camp. As the Indians proceeded toward this place, Smith separated from them and went southwest with Tontileaugo, his wife and children, Tecaughretanego, and his son Nunganey.

After some time one of Tontileaugo's stepsons, an eight-year-old boy, did something that offended him. When Tontileaugo punished the boy with a whipping, the child's mother was greatly incensed. In Tontileaugo's absence she took her children and all her possessions and started back to the Wyandot country. When Tontileaugo found she had gone he was disturbed and started after her. They met and made up their quarrel, but they did not return to their companions. Smith was left for the winter with Tecaughretanego and his son, who was about ten years old.

> Tecaughretanego had been a first-rate warrior, statesman, and hunter, and though he was now near sixty years of age, was yet equal to the common run of hunters, but subject to the rheumatism, which deprived him of the use of his legs.
>
> Shortly after Tontileaugo left us, Tecaughretanego became lame, and could scarcely walk out of our hut for two months. I had considerable success in hunting and trapping. Though Tecaughretanego endured much pain and misery, yet he bore it all with wonderful patience and would often endeavor to entertain me with cheerful conversation. Sometimes he would applaud me for my diligence, skill, and activity; and at other times he would take care in giving me instructions concerning the hunting and trapping business. He would also tell me that if I failed of success we would suffer very much, as we were about forty miles from anyone living, that we knew of; yet he would not intimate that he apprehended we were in any danger, but still supposed that I was fully adequate to the task.

Deer feeding in the snow

Things went well until February, when there came a snow with a crust. The noise of its breaking under a hunter's feet warned off the deer, and bear and beaver were scarce in this area. The three campers were entirely out of provisions. Smith hunted for two days without eating at all, but had no success. Discouraged, he returned to the winter cabin. Tecaughretanego reassured him, saying that "the great Being above feeds his people, and gives them their meat in due season." He told Smith that when he went hunting the following day, the Great Spirit would direct his way. Smith writes:

> The next morning I went out, and steered about an east course. I proceeded on slowly for about five miles, and saw deer frequently, but as the crust on the snow made a great noise they were always running before I spied them, so that I could not get a shot. A violent appetite returned, and I became intolerably hungry. It was now that I concluded I would run off to Pennsylvania, my native country. . . .
>
> I then proceeded on as fast as I could walk, and when I got about ten or twelve miles from our hut, I came upon fresh buffalo tracks; I pursued after, and in a short time came in sight of them as they were passing through a small glade. I ran with all my might and headed them, where I lay in ambush and killed a

very large cow. I immediately kindled a fire and began to roast meat; but could not wait till it was done; I ate it almost raw. When hunger was abated, I began to be tenderly concerned for my old Indian brother and the little boy I had left in a perishing condition. I made haste and packed up what meat I could carry, secured what I left from the wolves, and returned homewards.

I scarcely thought of the old man's speech while I was almost distracted with hunger, but on my return was much affected with it, reflected on myself for my hard-heartedness and ingratitude in attempting to run off and leave the venerable old man and little boy to perish with hunger. I also considered how remarkably the old man's speech had been verified in our providentially obtaining a supply.

Smith had great respect and admiration for Tecaughretanego and writes that he was "no common person," but like a Socrates among the Indians.

In April, Tecaughretanego had sufficiently recovered so that he could walk. The three campers made a birchbark canoe and eventually reached the Wyandot town they had left the previous fall. Three days later they left for Detroit, where they spent the summer. The next winter they traveled nearly the same route they had during the previous hunting season. They had considerable success and returned to Detroit in April, 1759.

Shortly after this, Tecaughretanego, his son Nunganey, and myself went from Detroit (in an elm-bark canoe) to Caughnegawa, a very ancient Indian town, about nine miles above Montreal, where I remained until about the first of July. I then heard of a French ship at Montreal that had English prisoners on board in order to carry them oversea and exchange them. I went privately off from the Indians and got also on board; but as General Wolfe had stopped the river St. Lawrence we were all sent to prison in Montreal, where I remained four months. Some time in November we were all sent off from this place to Crown Point, and exchanged.

Early in the year 1760 I came home to Conococheague and found that my people could never ascertain whether I was killed or taken until my return. They received me with great joy, but were surprised to see me so much like an Indian both in my gait and gesture.

Smith had been in captivity for over four years; during this time he had learned much about the Indians. When, in 1763, war with the tribes broke out along the Pennsylvania frontier, he and two subordinates who had also been captives trained troops to fight in the Indian way. The men had some success in protecting the frontier.

In 1776, Smith was appointed a major in the Pennsylvania revolutionary troops. In 1777 he and his men fought the British in New Jersey. In 1788 he settled in Bourbon County, Kentucky, where he was elected as a member of the convention that conferred about a separation from the state of Virginia.

And from that year until 1799 I represented Bourbon County either in convention or as a member of the general assembly, except two years when I was left a few votes behind.

MARY JEMISON

Mary Jemison was one of the captives who chose to live out her life among the Indians, for reasons that she gives in her narrative. Her adult years were spent among the Senecas near Geneseo, New York, where she eventually owned a large piece of land on the Gardow flats. She had taken care not to forget the English language and spoke English frequently to white neighbors near her home.

When she was eighty years old she told her story to James Seaver, who wrote it down. Seaver describes her as a short little woman with a very white skin, blue eyes, and hair formerly a light chestnut brown, but then turning quite gray. People who knew her agreed that she must have been beautiful in her youth. At eighty, she had an alert, happy disposition and a remarkable memory. She was still very active, performing the farm chores of gathering and chopping wood, feeding her cattle and poultry, and planting, tending, and harvesting corn. At the time she told her story to Seaver she still lived on the Gardow flats, although later she moved.

Her parents were Irish emigrants to America. In 1742 they

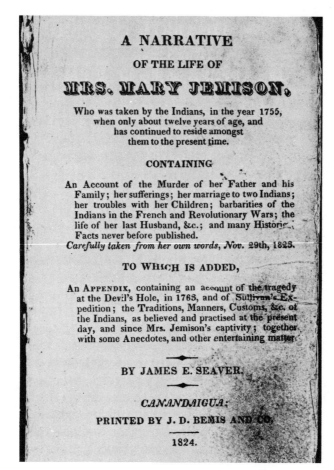

Title page of the original edition of Mary Jemison's story

had set sail for Philadelphia on the ship *William and Mary*, with their three children, two sons and a daughter. Mary was born during the voyage.

Thomas Jemison, Mary's father, took the family to the Pennsylvania frontier, to a tract of excellent land lying on Marsh Creek. Here he cleared a large farm and prospered. Two more sons were born to the Jemisons during this time.

At the outbreak of the French and Indian War in 1755, life along the frontier became hazardous, but Jemison was reluctant to move. His farm remained free of Indian attack until April, 1758.

On April 4, 1758, Mary, then fifteen years old, was sent to

a neighbor's house about a mile away to get a horse and return with it the next morning. That evening as she walked out into the neighbor's yard she saw what she thought was a white sheet, widespread, approaching her. She imagined she was caught in it and fell to the ground, unconscious. The neighbors had difficulty in reviving her, but she had recovered by morning. In later years she interpreted the appearance of the sheet as a foreboding of the disaster that was to overtake her family.

When Mary returned home with the horse in the morning she found that another neighbor, a man, with his sister-in-law and her three children, had come to live with the Jemisons for a while. She was never certain of the reason for this visit. She continued her narrative as follows:

> Immediately after I got home, the man took the horse to go to his house after a bag of grain, and took his gun in his hand for the purpose of killing game, if he should chance to see any. Our family, as usual, was busily employed about their common business. Father was shaving an axe-helve at the side of the house; mother was making preparations for breakfast; my two oldest brothers were at work near the barn; and the little ones, with myself, and the woman and her three children, were in the house.
>
> Breakfast was not yet ready when we were alarmed by the discharge of a number of guns that seemed to be near. Mother and the woman before mentioned almost fainted at the report, and everyone trembled with fear. On opening the door, the man and horse lay dead near the house, having just been shot by the Indians.
>
> I was afterwards informed that the Indians discovered him at his own house with his gun, and pursued him to father's, where they shot him as I have related. They first secured my father, and then rushed into the house and without the least resistance made prisoners of my mother, Robert, Matthew, Betsey, the woman and her three children, and myself, and then commenced plundering.
>
> My two brothers Thomas and John, being at the barn, escaped and went to Virginia, where my grandfather Erwin then lived, as I was informed by a Mr. Fields, who was at my house about the close of the Revolutionary War.

The party that took us consisted of six Indians and four Frenchmen, who immediately commenced plundering . . . and took what they considered most valuable, consisting principally of bread, meal, and meat. Having taken as much provisions as they could carry, they set out with their prisoners in great haste, for fear of detection, and soon entered the woods. On our march that day an Indian went behind us with a whip, with which he frequently lashed the children to make them keep up. In this manner we traveled till dark without a mouthful of food or a drop of water, although we had not eaten since the night before.

The company arose at dawn the next day and again began their march. At about sunrise they halted and the Indians gave their captives a large breakfast made up of provisions taken from the Jemison house. After breakfast the party continued on its way.

Towards evening we arrived at the border of a dark and dismal swamp, which was covered with small hemlocks, or some other evergreen, and other bushes, into which we were conducted; and having gone a short distance we stopped to encamp for the night.

Here we had some bread and meat for supper; but the dreariness of our situation, together with the uncertainty under which we all labored as to our future destiny, almost deprived us of the sense of hunger, and destroyed our relish for food.

Mother, from the time we were taken, had manifested a great degree of fortitude, and encouraged us to support our troubles without complaining; and by her conversation seemed to make the distance and time shorter and the way more smooth. But father lost all his ambition in the beginning of our trouble, and continued apparently lost to every care—absorbed in melancholy. Here, as before, she insisted on the necessity of our eating; and we obeyed her, but it was done with heavy hearts.

As soon as I had finished my supper, an Indian took off my shoes and stockings and put a pair of moccasins on my feet, which my mother observed; and believing that they [the Indians] would spare my life, even if they should destroy the other captives, addressed me as near as I can remember in the following words:

"My dear little Mary, I fear that the time has arrived when we must be parted forever. Your life, my child, I think will be spared; but we shall probably be tomahawked here in this lonesome place by the Indians. Oh! how can I part with you, my darling? . . . Alas, my dear! my heart bleeds at the thoughts of what awaits you; but if you leave us, remember my child your own name and the name of your father and mother. Be careful and not forget your English tongue. If you shall have an opportunity to get away from the Indians, don't try to escape; for if you do they will find and destroy you. Don't forget, my little daughter, the prayers that I have learned you—say them often; be a good child, and God will bless you. May God bless you, my child, and make you comfortable and happy."

The Indian also put moccasins on one of the neighbor's sons and led the boy and girl away into the woods. There they spent the night. Mary Jemison never saw her family again. The next morning the Indians and Frenchmen who had been left behind the night before joined the children and their guardian, but there was no sign of the other captives. Mary suspected they had been scalped, but she dared not express her feelings by crying; she could not inquire for her parents because she did not speak the Indians' language, nor they hers. "My only relief," she says, "was in silent, stifled sobs."

Having given the little boy and myself some bread and meat for breakfast, they led us on as fast as we could travel, and one of them went behind and with a long staff, picked up all the grass and weeds that we trailed down by going over them. By taking that precaution they avoided detection; for each weed was so nicely placed in its natural position that no one would have suspected that we had passed that way. It is the custom of Indians when scouting, or on private expeditions, to step carefully and where no impression of their feet can be left—shunning wet or muddy ground. They seldom take hold of a bush or limb, and never break one; and by observing those precautions and that of setting up the weeds and grass which they necessarily lop, they completely elude the sagacity of their pursuers.

That night the Indians encamped in a thicket, where they made a shelter of boughs and built a good fire so that everyone could get warm and dry out their clothing, for the day had been rainy. There Mary's worst suspicions were confirmed. After everyone had eaten, the Indians took fresh scalps from their baggage and began drying them and preparing them against spoilage. Mary could not avoid seeing the Indians at work nor could she avoid noticing the color of the hair. Her mother's bright red hair and the hair of her father and of her two younger brothers and her sister were easily recognizable. The sight was appalling to her, yet of necessity she had to endure it without complaining.

The next morning the Indians continued their march. They traveled through a continual fall of rain and snow for two days, then because of the storm they remained in their camp for the next two days. When the weather cleared, the company went on, to arrive that afternoon at Fort Duquesne. Outside the enclosure the Indians halted while they combed the hair of their captives and painted their faces and hair red, "in the finest Indian style." The captives were then conducted into the fort. The next day, the boy and a young man who had also been captured were given to the French.

> I was now left alone in the fort, deprived of my former companions and of everything that was near or dear to me in life. But it was not long before I was in some measure relieved by the appearance of two pleasant-looking squaws of the Seneca tribe who came and examined me attentively for a short time, and then went out. After a few minutes' absence they returned with my former masters, who gave me to them to dispose of as they pleased. . . .
>
> My former Indian masters and the two squaws were soon ready to leave the fort, and accordingly embarked; the Indians in a large canoe, and the two squaws and myself in a small one, and went down the Ohio. . . .
>
> At night we arrived at a small Seneca Indian town, at the mouth of a small river that was called by the Indians, in the Seneca language, Shenanjee, where the two squaws to whom I belonged resided. There we landed and the Indians went on; which was the last I ever saw of them.
>
> Having made fast to the shore, the squaws left me in the canoe while they went to their wigwam or house in the town and returned with a suit of Indian clothing, all new, and very clean and nice. My clothes, though whole and good when I was

taken, were now torn in pieces, so that I was almost naked. They first undressed me and threw my rags into the river; then washed me clean and dressed me in the new suit they had just brought, in complete Indian style; and then led me home and seated me in the center of their wigwam.

I had been in that situation but a few minutes before all the squaws in the town came in to see me. I was soon surrounded by them, and they immediately set up a most dismal howling, crying bitterly and wringing their hands in all the agonies of grief for a deceased relative.

Their tears flowed freely and they exhibited all the signs of real mourning. At the commencement of this scene, one of their number began, in a voice somewhat between speaking and singing, to recite some words to the following purport, and continued the recitation till the ceremony was ended; the company at the same time varying the appearance of their countenances, gestures, and tone of voice, so as to correspond with the sentiments expressed by their leader:

"Oh, our brother! Alas! He is dead—he has gone; he will never return! Friendless he died on the field of the slain, where his bones are yet lying unburied! Oh, who will not mourn his sad fate? No tears dropped around him; oh, no! No tears of his sisters were there! He fell in his prime, when his arm was most needed to keep us from danger! Alas! he has gone! and left us in sorrow, his loss to bewail. Oh, where is his spirit? . . . Though he fell on the field of the slain, with glory he fell, and his spirit went up to the land of his fathers in war! Then why do we mourn? With transports of joy they received him, and fed him, and clothed him, and welcomed him there! Oh, friends, he is happy; then dry up your tears! His spirit has seen our distress, and sent us a helper whom with pleasure we greet. Dickewamis has come; then let us receive her with joy! She is handsome and pleasant! Oh! she is our sister, and gladly we welcome her here. In the place of our brother she stands in our tribe. With care we will guard her from trouble; and may she be happy till her spirit shall leave us."

In the course of that ceremony, from mourning they became serene—joy sparkled in their countenances, and they seemed to rejoice over me as over a long-lost child. I was made welcome amongst them as a sister to the two squaws before

mentioned, and was called Dickewamis; which being interpreted, signifies a pretty girl, a handsome girl, or a pleasant,
good thing. That is the name by which I have ever since been
called by the Indians.

It was not until later, after Mary learned the Indians' language, that she was able to find out what had been said on this
occasion.

I afterwards learned that the ceremony I at that time passed
through was that of adoption. The two squaws had lost a
brother in Washington's war, sometime in the year before, and
in consequence of this death went up to Fort Pitt [Duquesne]
on the day that I arrived there, in order to receive a prisoner or
an enemy's scalp, to supply their loss.

It is a custom of the Indians, when one of their number is
slain or taken prisoner in battle, to give to the nearest relative to
the dead or absent a prisoner, if they have chanced to take one,
and if not, to give him the scalp of an enemy. On the return of
the Indians from conquest, which is always announced by pecu-
liar shoutings, demonstrations of joy, and the exhibition of
some trophy of victory, the mourners come forward and make
their claims. If they receive a prisoner, it is at their option either
to satiate their vengeance by taking his life in the most cruel
manner they can conceive of; or to receive and adopt him into
the family, in the place of him whom they have lost. All the
prisoners that are taken in battle and carried to the encampment or town by the Indians are given to the bereaved families
till their number is made good. And unless the mourners have
but just received news of their bereavement and are under the
operation of a paroxysm of grief, anger, and revenge; or unless
the prisoner is very old, sickly, or homely, they generally save
him and treat him kindly. . . .

It was my happy lot to be accepted for adoption; and at
the time of the ceremony I was received by the two squaws to
supply the place of their brother in the family; and I was ever
considered and treated by them as a real sister, the same as
though I had been born of their mother. . . .

Being now settled and provided with a home, I was
employed in nursing the children and doing light work about
the house. Occasionally I was sent out with the Indian hunters,

when they went but a short distance, to help them carry their game. My situation was easy; I had no particular hardships to endure. But still, the recollection of my parents, my brothers and sister, my home, and my own captivity, destroyed my happiness, and made me constantly solitary, lonesome, and gloomy.

My sisters would not allow me to speak English in their hearing; but remembering the charge that my dear mother gave me at the time I left her, whenever I chanced to be alone I made a business of repeating my prayer, catechism, or something I had learned, in order that I might not forget my own language. By practicing in that way I retained it till I came to Genesee flats, where I soon became acquainted with English people with whom I have been almost daily in the habit of conversing.

My sisters were diligent in teaching me their language; and to their great satisfaction I soon learned so that I could understand it readily and speak it fluently. I was very fortunate in falling into their hands; for they were kind, good-natured women; peaceable and mild in their dispositions; temperate and decent in their habits, and very tender and gentle towards me. I have great reason to respect them, though they have been dead a great number of years.

The Indians spent the summer raising their crops at the village where Mary's adopted sisters lived. When the winter came, they moved to quarters farther down the Ohio River. In the spring they returned to the village at the mouth of the river Shenanjee. There they again planted their corn, squashes, and beans on the fields that were used the preceding summer.

At about this time, apparently, the British had taken over Fort Duquesne and had renamed it Fort Pitt.

About planting time, our Indians all went up to Fort Pitt to make peace with the British, and took me with them. We landed on the opposite side of the river from the fort, and encamped for the night. Early the next morning the Indians took me over to the fort to see the white people that were there. It was then that my heart bounded to be liberated from the Indians and to be restored to my friends and my country. The white people were surprised to see me with the Indians, enduring the hardships of a savage life at so early an age, and with so

delicate a constitution as I appeared to possess. They asked me
my name; where and when I was taken—and appeared very
much interested on my behalf. They were continuing their
inquiries when my sisters became alarmed, believing that I
should be taken from them, hurried me into their canoe and
recrossed the river—took their bread out of the fire and fled
with me, without stopping, till they arrived at the river Shenanjee. So great was their fear of losing me or of my being given up
in the treaty that they never once stopped rowing till they got
home.

Shortly after we left the shore opposite the fort, as I was
informed by one of my Indian brothers, the white people came
over to take me back; but after considerable inquiry, and having
made diligent search to find where I was hid, they returned with
heavy hearts. Although I had then been with the Indians something over a year, and had become considerably habituated to
their mode of living, and attached to my sisters, the sight of
white people who could speak English inspired me with an
unspeakable anxiety to go home with them and share in the
blessings of civilization. My sudden departure and escape from
them seemed like a second captivity, and for a long time I
brooded the thoughts of my miserable situation with almost as
much sorrow and dejection as I had done those of my first sufferings. Time, the destroyer of every affection, wore away my
unpleasant feelings and I became as contented as before.

At the end of the summer the Indians went to their winter
quarters. Early in the spring they went up the Ohio River to a
place the Indians called Wiishto where, on either side, a stream
emptied into the larger river. There they built a new town in
which they lived for three years, returning to their old winter
site each fall. The first summer they lived at Wiishto a party
of Delaware Indians joined them. They brought five prisoners
with whom Mary became friendly. "[They] made my situation
much more agreeable as they could all speak English," she says.

Not long after the Delawares came to live with us at Wiishto
my sisters told me that I must go and live with one of them,
whose name was Sheninjee. Not daring to cross them or disobey
their commands, with a great degree of reluctance I went; and
Sheninjee and I were married according to Indian custom.

Sheninjee was a noble man; large in stature; elegant in his appearance; generous in his conduct; courageous in war; a friend to peace, and a great lover of justice. He supported a degree of dignity far above his rank, and merited and received the confidence and friendship of all the tribes with whom he was acquainted. Yet Sheninjee was an Indian. The idea of spending my days with him at first seemed perfectly irreconcilable to my feelings; but his good nature, generosity, tenderness, and friendship towards me soon gained my affection; and strange as it may seem, I loved him. To me he was ever kind in sickness and always treated me with gentleness; in fact, he was an agreeable husband and a comfortable companion. We lived happily together till the time of our final separation, which happened two or three years after our marriage, as I shall presently relate.

In the second summer at Wiishto, Mary Jemison gave birth to a baby daughter, who lived only two days, to her mother's great sorrow.

From that time, nothing remarkable occurred to me till the fourth winter of my captivity when I had a son born, while I was at Sciota [the winter quarters]; I had a quick recovery, and my child was healthy. To commemorate the name of my much lamented father, I called my son Thomas Jemison. . . .

In the spring when Thomas was three or four months old, we set out to go to Fort Pitt, to dispose of our fur and skins that we had taken during the winter and procure some necessary articles for the use of our family.

I had been with the Indians four summers and four winters and had become so far accustomed to their mode of living, habits, and disposition that my anxiety to get away and leave them had almost subsided. With them was my home; my family was there, and there I had many friends to whom I was warmly attached in consideration of the favors, affection, and friendship with which they had uniformly treated me from the time of my adoption. Our labor was not severe. . . . Notwithstanding the Indian women have all the fuel and bread to procure and the cooking to perform, their task is probably not harder than that of white women, who have those articles provided for them; and their cares certainly are not half as numerous nor as great. In the summer season we planted, tended, and har-

The method by which Mary Jemison carried her son Thomas to Fort Pitt

vested our corn, and generally had all our children with us; but had no master to oversee or drive us, so we would work as leisurely as we pleased. We had no plows on the Ohio, but performed the whole process of planting and hoeing with a small tool that resembled, in some respects, a hoe with a very short handle.

Our cooking consisted in pounding our corn into samp or hominy, boiling the hominy, making now and then a cake and baking it in the ashes, and in boiling or roasting our venison. As our cooking and eating utensils consisted of a hominy block and pestle, a small kettle, a knife or two, and a few vessels of bark or wood, it required but little time to keep them in order of use. . . .

In the season of hunting it was our business, in addition to our cooking, to bring home the game that was taken by the Indians, dress it, and carefully preserve the eatable meat, and prepare and dress the skins. Our clothing was fastened together with strings of deer skin, and tied on with the same.

In that manner we lived without any of those jealousies, quarrels, and revengeful battles between families and individuals which have become common in the Indian tribes since the introduction of ardent spirits among them.

The use of ardent spirits amongst the Indians, and the attempts which have been made to civilize and christianize them by the white people has constantly made them worse and worse. . . .

Notwithstanding all that has been said against the Indians, in consequence of their cruelties to their enemies—cruelties that I have witnessed and had abundant proof of—it is a fact that they are naturally kind, tender, and peaceable toward their friends, and strictly honest, and that those cruelties have been practiced only upon their enemies, according to their idea of justice.

The company with whom Mary Jemison traveled to Fort Pitt consisted of her husband, her two Indian brothers, and her son. They said good-by to friends in their village with regret, as they thought it probable that they would not return for some time. Instead, they had half decided to visit a part of their family who lived at Genishau, on the Genesee River in New York. These relatives had frequently sent them invitations.

After trading, the small company encamped for the summer. During that time one of the brothers who had been with the people at Genishau arrived with another invitation. Because he was so insistent, the two brothers from Wiishto definitely decided to go to Genishau and to take Mary and her son with them. Summer was now almost over and they wished to set out at once, for fear the autumn rains might overtake them. Sheninjee agreed to Mary's going, but he wished to spend the winter in hunting and said he would join his wife in the spring.

Mary, her son, and her three adopted brothers started eastward to Genishau, a Seneca village that was southwest of the present city of Geneseo, New York. Here they were kindly received by a woman whom Mary Jemison calls "my Indian mother" and by other members of the family.

I spent the winter comfortably, and as agreeably as I could have expected to, in the absence of my kind husband. Spring at length appeared, but my husband had not found me. Fearful forebodings haunted my imagination; yet I felt confident that his affection for me was so great that if he was alive he would follow me and I should again see him. In the course of the summer, however, I received intelligence that soon after he left me at Yishahwana he was taken sick and died at Wiishto. This was a heavy and an unexpected blow. I was now in my youthful days left a widow, with one son, and entirely dependent on myself for his and my support. My mother and her family gave me all the consolation in their power, and in a few months my grief wore off and I became contented.

A year or two after this the English Government offered a bounty to anyone who would return prisoners taken by the Indians during the war between the English and the French. A Dutchman who had been at Genishau decided to take Mary to the British at Niagara and receive the money offered. She watched him carefully in order to avoid falling into his hands. One day he approached her when she was working alone in a cornfield. She saw him coming and ran to an old cabin some distance away. There she remained for three days until she was sure it was safe to return home. After this episode, the council of chiefs gave orders that she was not to be taken to any military post without her consent, but should be allowed to live among the Indians undisturbed.

The old king of the tribe, however, told one of Mary's brothers that he himself would redeem Mary to the British and receive the money. At that, the brother replied that if Mary were in danger of being taken by force he would kill her with his own hands. Mary's Indian sister was distraught when she heard this, for she knew her brother spoke in dead earnest.

> Full of pity and anxious for my preservation, she then directed me to take my child and go into some high weeds at no great distance from the house, and there hide myself and lay still till all was silent in the house, for my brother, she said, would return at evening and let her know the final conclusion of the matter, of which she promised to inform me in the following manner: If I was to be killed, she said she would bake a small

cake and lay it at the door on the outside, in a place that she then pointed out to me. When all was silent in the house, I was to creep softly to the door, and if the cake could not be found in the place specified, I was to go in; but if the cake was there, I was to take my child and go as fast as I possibly could to a large spring on the south side of Samp's Creek (a place that I had often seen) and there wait till I should by some means hear from her.

Alarmed for my own safety, I instantly followed her advice and went into the weeds, where I lay in a state of the greatest anxiety till all was silent in the house, when I crept to the door, and there found, to my great distress, the little cake! I knew my fate was fixed unless I could keep secreted till the storm was over; and accordingly crept back to the weeds, where my little Thomas lay, took him on my back, and laid my course for the spring as fast as my legs would carry me. Thomas was nearly three years old, and very large and heavy. I got to the spring early in the morning, almost overcome with fatigue; and at the same time, fearing that I might be pursued and taken, I felt my life an almost insupportable burthen. I sat down with my child at the spring, and he and I made a breakfast of the little cake, and water of the spring. . . .

In the morning after I fled, as was expected, the old king came to our house in search of me, and to take me off; but, as I was not to be found, he gave me up and went to Niagara with the prisoners he had already got into his possession.

As soon as the king had gone, Mary's brother came to take her home. From then on she lived peaceably among the Indians. When Thomas was about four years old, she was married to an Indian named Hickatoo. They eventually had four daughters and two sons, all of whom Mary named for English relatives she remembered.

After the conflict between the French and the British was over, the Indians lived quietly until the American Revolution. For many years there was no warfare, but the men kept up their military skills by indulging in mimic battles on special feast days. They also practiced various athletic games—running, wrestling, leaping, and playing ball to keep their bodies in good shape.

During the Revolution the Seneca town was completely

destroyed by General Sullivan's troops. The houses were set afire, the corn was burned and thrown into the river, the cattle and horses were killed, and the fruit trees were destroyed. Nothing was left but bare soil and timber. The Indians had fled before the devastation took place; when they returned, winter was coming on.

> The weather by this time had become cold and stormy; and as we were destitute of houses and food too, I immediately resolved to take my children and look out for myself, without delay. With this intention I took two of my little ones on my back, bade the other three follow, and the same night arrived on the Gardow flats, where I have since resided.

> At that time, two Negroes, who had run away from their masters some time before, were the only inhabitants of these flats. They lived in a small cabin and had planted and raised a large field of corn, which they had not yet harvested. As they were in want of help to secure their crop, I hired to them to husk corn till the whole was harvested. . . .

> I husked enough for them to gain for myself, at every tenth string, one hundred strings of ears, which were equal to twenty-five bushels of shelled corn. This seasonable supply made my family comfortable for samp and cakes through the succeeding winter, which was the most severe that I have witnessed since my remembrance. The snow fell about five feet deep, and remained so for a long time, and the weather was extremely cold; so much so, indeed, that almost all the game upon which the Indians depended for subsistence, perished, and reduced them almost to a state of starvation through that and three or four succeeding years. . . .

> The Negroes continued on the flats two or three years after this, and then left them for a place that they expected would suit them much better. But as that land became my own in a few years, by virtue of a deed from the chiefs of the Six Nations, I have lived there from that to the present time.

Soon after the Revolution, one of Mary's brothers offered her liberty and the chance to go back to her white relatives. Her son Thomas was anxious that she should go and offered to accompany her on the journey, to take care of the younger children and to provide food as they traveled through the wilderness.

Thomas had qualities that might make him an outstanding man; because of the promise he showed, the chiefs of the tribe were unwilling to let him go.

> To go myself, and leave him, was more than I felt able to do; for he had been kind to me, and was one on whom I placed great dependence. The chiefs' refusing to let him go was one reason for my resolving to stay; but another, more powerful, if possible, was that I had got a large family of Indian children, that I must take with me; and that if I should be so fortunate as to find my relatives, they would despise them, if not myself; and treat us as enemies; or at least with a degree of cold indifference, which I thought I could not endure.
>
> Accordingly, after I had duly considered the matter, I told my brother that it was my choice to stay and spend the remainder of my days with my Indian friends, and live with my family as I had heretofore done. He appeared well pleased with my resolution, and informed me that as that was my choice, I should have a piece of land that I could call my own, where I could live unmolested, and have something at my decease to leave for the benefit of my children.

When the great council of Indian chiefs met in 1797, Mary Jemison was granted a deed to the huge piece of land called Gardow flats, as she previously mentioned. This ground was very fertile, and much too large an area for the Jemison family to cultivate by themselves. Accordingly, Mary Jemison was given permission to lease some of the land to white people in the area who would farm it on shares. This arrangement supplied her and her family with a comfortable living.

In general, the Jemison children were friendly to each other and their mother had little difficulty with them when they were small. There was one source of trouble, however. From the time he was quite young, Thomas, the eldest, called his brother John a witch. As the two boys grew older this matter caused severe quarrels between them. When they became men, John married two wives. Polygamy was permitted in the tribe, but Thomas was very much against it. He constantly reprimanded John, telling him that his conduct was beneath the dignity of a good Indian.

John always resented such reprimand and reproof with a great degree of passion, though they never quarreled unless Thomas was intoxicated.

In his fits of drunkenness, Thomas seemed to lose all his natural reason and to conduct [himself] like a wild or crazy man, without regard to relatives, decency, or propriety. . . .

For a number of years their difficulties, and consequent unhappiness, continued and rather increased, continually exciting in my breast the most fearful apprehensions and greatest anxiety for their safety. With tears in my eyes I advised them to become reconciled to each other and to be friendly. . . .

My advice and expostulation with my sons were abortive; and year after year their disaffection for each other increased. At length, Thomas came to my house on the 1st day of July, 1811, in my absence, somewhat intoxicated, where he found John, with whom he immediately commenced a quarrel on their old subjects of difference. John's anger became desperate. He caught Thomas by the hair of his head, dragged him out at the door and there killed him, by a blow which he gave him on the head with a tomahawk.

When Mary Jemison returned and found Thomas murdered by the hand of his brother she was overcome with grief. As soon as she recovered enough to think of the situation she requested the chiefs to hold a council and "dispose of John as they should think proper." John, fearful of the punishment he might receive, fled to Canada.

When the chiefs had considered the matter carefully, they decided that Thomas had been the "first transgressor, and that for the abuses which he had offered he had merited from John the treatment that he had received." John, upon learning of his acquittal by the council, returned to his family.

In November, 1811, Mary Jemison's husband, Hickatoo, died. He had been ill for four years with tuberculosis. As nearly as can be estimated, he was one hundred and three years old at the time of his death. In his younger years he had been a great warrior, although one of almost unparalleled cruelty. While admitting his fierce nature in combat, Mary Jemison testifies to his gentle and generous conduct with friends. Hickatoo was buried with the insignia of a veteran warrior—a war club, a tomahawk, a scalping knife, a powder flask, flint, a piece of spunk, a small cake, and a cup.

More grief was not long in coming. The two remaining sons, John and Jesse, had a quarrel while both were intoxicated. The outcome was that John killed Jesse, who was the youngest child and, Mary Jemison admits, her favorite and the one most helpful to her.

Jesse shunned the company of his brothers and the Indians generally, and never attended their frolics; and it was supposed that this, together with my partiality for him, were the causes which excited in John so great a degree of envy that nothing short of death would satisfy it.

As Mary Jemison remarks in her memoirs, "Trouble seldom comes single." John was to cause her further anguish.

My son John was a doctor, considerably celebrated amongst the Indians of various tribes for his skill in curing their diseases by the administration of roots and herbs, which he gathered in the forests and other places where they had been planted by the hand of nature.

In the month of April, or first of May, 1817, he was called upon to go to Buffalo, Cattaraugus, and Allegheny, to cure some who were sick. He went, and was absent about two months. When he returned, he observed the Great Slide of the bank of Genesee River, a short distance above my house, which had taken place during his absence; and conceiving that circumstance to be ominous of his own death, called at his sister Nancy's, told her that he should live but a few days, and wept bitterly at the near approach of his dissolution. Nancy endeavored to persuade him that his trouble was imaginary, and that he ought not to be affected by a fancy which was visionary. Her arguments were ineffectual and afforded no alleviation to his mental sufferings. From his sister's he went to his own house, where he stayed only two nights, and then went to Squawky Hill to procure money with which to purchase flour for the use of his family.

While John was at Squawky Hill he engaged in a drinking bout with two other Indians. The spree ended in a violent quar-

Statue of Mary Jemison, who became known as the "white woman of the Genesee"

rel during which John's two companions set upon him and beat out his brains. All three of Mary Jemison's sons had now died violently. Their loss robbed her of a good deal of the happiness which she had looked forward to enjoying in her later years.

Mary Jemison's land had been sought by various schemers who hoped to defraud her of it. In the winter of 1822–23 she received the permission of the chiefs and of the United States Commissioner of Indian Lands to sell legally all but a tract on the riverbank two miles long and one mile wide, which she kept.

In 1825 the Senecas sold their tribal lands on the Genesee River to white settlers. The Indians moved their families to New

York reservations, and Mary Jemison and her daughters with their families were left surrounded by white neighbors. Six years later, Mary, lonesome for her Indian friends and kindred, decided to join them. She sold her remaining two square miles of land and moved to the Buffalo Creek reservation, where she purchased Indian possessary rights to a good farm. Here she lived in peace until her death in September, 1833, when she was about ninety-one years old. Even in old age she had remained alert, good-natured, and exuberant. Shortly before her death, remembering her mother's urgings not to forget her prayers, she became a Christian. She was buried near the Seneca Mission church at Buffalo Creek, but years later, under the direction of one of her grandsons, her remains were removed to the Genesee River, to an area that is now a state public park—Letchworth Park.

JOHN TANNER

John Tanner was seized by an Indian raiding party in Kentucky in 1789, when he was not quite eleven years old. He lived with the Ottawa and Ojibway Indians for almost thirty years. During that time he never gave up the idea of going back to his own people; in 1817 he made the journey to Kentucky for a reunion with his relatives. His long residence among the Indians appears to have made it difficult for him to adjust to another way of living, however, and he eventually returned north and became an interpreter for the Indian agent at Sault Sainte Marie.

It is impossible to know what sort of person Tanner might have become if he had not suddenly been transplanted from one culture to another at an early age. As it was, he seems to have been a misfit both among the Indians and among the whites. Apparently he had a deep-seated suspicion of other people's motives and possessed a fiery temper that often led to violence. In many of his actions he followed the Indian way as he understood it. "An Indian always expects any outrage he commits shall be retaliated according to their customs, and a man who omits to take proper revenge is but lightly esteemed among them," he

John Tanner

said. His story of his life among the Indians is full of quarrels, often of his own making. In later years the whites at Sault Sainte Marie thought him a man to fear.

Tanner's narrative is a long and detailed one, with a background of the region around the Great Lakes and the Red River and Assinneboine River of Canada. Among the Indians with whom he lived, fur trading was the chief means of subsistence. Winters were spent in hunting and trapping. In the spring came the visit to the trading posts, with its almost inevitable long alcoholic debauch. Like many of the other captives among the Indians, Tanner recognized and deplored the terrible toll that the white culture was taking in introducing alcohol and disease among the Indians and in disrupting their customary patterns of living. Again and again his narrative reveals the Indians' dependence on the fur traders. Some of the traders, it is true, realized their responsibilities and in times of want and famine did what they could to help the Indians. The picture of the trading posts and their agents and of the rivalry between the Northwest Company and the Hudson's Bay Company is a valuable part of Tanner's narrative, as are also his closely observed accounts of tribal customs and traditions. He told his story orally to Edwin James, who wrote it down.

Tanner's father was a farmer from Virginia who had been a clergyman. Young John's earliest recollection was the death of his mother when he was two years old. Soon after that the family moved to a place called Elk Horn, where his father married again. Tanner says:

> I cannot tell how long we remained at Elk Horn; when we moved, we traveled two days with horses and wagons, and came to the Ohio, where my father bought three flat boats; the sides of these boats had bullet holes in them, and there was blood on them, which I understood was that of people who had been killed by the Indians. In one of these boats we put the horses and cattle—in another, beds, furniture, and other property, and in the third were some Negroes. The cattle boat and the family boat were lashed together; the third, with the Negroes, followed behind. We descended the Ohio, and in two or three days came to Cincinnati. . . .
>
> In one day we went from Cincinnati to the mouth of the Big Miami, opposite which we were to settle. Here was some cleared land, and one or two log cabins, but they had been deserted on account of the Indians. My father rebuilt the cabins, and enclosed them with a strong picket. It was early in the spring when we arrived at the mouth of the Big Miami, and we were soon engaged in preparing a field to plant corn. I think it was not more than ten days after our arrival when my father told us in the morning that from the actions of the horses he perceived there were Indians lurking about in the woods, and he said to me, "John, you must not go out of the house today." After giving strict charge to my stepmother to let none of the

little children go out, he went to the field with the Negroes and my elder brother, to drop corn.

John was told to take care of the youngest child, but he soon became bored.

I watched my opportunity and escaped into the yard; thence through a small door in the large gate of the wall into the open field. There was a walnut tree at some distance from the house and near the side of the field, where I had been in the habit of finding some of the last year's nuts. To gain this tree without being seen by my father and those in the field, I had to use some precaution. I remember perfectly well having seen my father as I skulked towards the tree; he stood in the middle of the field, with the gun in his hand, to watch for Indians, while the others were dropping corn. As I came near the tree I thought to myself, "I wish I could see these Indians." I had partly filled with nuts a straw hat which I wore when I heard a crackling noise behind me; I looked around and saw the Indians; almost at the same instant I was seized by both hands and dragged off betwixt two. One of them took my straw hat, emptied the nuts on the ground, and put it on my head. The Indians who seized me were an old man and a young one; these were, as I learned subsequently, Manito-e-geezhik and his son Kish-kau-ko.

Later, Tanner learned that the wife of the old man, Manito-e-geezhik, had recently lost by death her youngest son; she complained bitterly to her husband that she could not live unless the boy were returned to her. Manito-e-geezhik understood her complaints as a hint that he was to bring her a captive whom she might adopt in her son's place. The old man and his companions had traveled from Lake Huron for the sole purpose of finding a suitable boy. John Tanner had stepped from his father's log cabin at the most opportune moment for them.

It was about one mile from my father's house to the place where they threw me into a hickory bark canoe, which was concealed under the bushes on the bank of the river. Into this they all seven jumped and immediately crossed the Ohio, landing at the mouth of the Big Miami and on the south side of that river.

Here they abandoned their canoe and stuck their paddles in the ground so that they could be seen from the river. At a little distance in the woods they had some blankets and provisions concealed; they offered me some dry venison and bear's grease, but I could not eat. My father's house was plainly to be seen from the place where we stood; they pointed at it, looked at me, and laughed, but I have never known what they said.

After they had eaten a little, they began to ascend the Miami, dragging me along as before. The shoes I had on when at home they took off, as they seemed to think I could run better without them. Although I perceived I was closely watched, all hope of escape did not immediately forsake me. As they hurried me along I endeavored, without their knowledge, to take notice of such objects as would serve as landmarks on my way back. I tried also, where I passed long grass or soft ground, to leave my tracks. I hoped to be able to escape after they should have fallen asleep at night. When night came, they lay down, placing me between the old man and Kish-kau-ko, so close together that the same blanket covered all three. I was so fatigued that I fell asleep immediately, and did not wake until sunrise next morning, when the Indians were up and ready to proceed on their journey. Thus we journeyed for about four days, the Indians hurrying me on, and I continuing to hope that I might escape, but still every night completely overpowered by sleep.

At last they came to a river so deep that the water was up to the Indians' armpits. Young John was carried across on the old man's shoulders. The boy knew he would not be able to return across the river alone, and he gave up all hope of immediate escape.

The party had been journeying for about fourteen days when they came to a place where there were some traders who spoke English. They talked with the boy and wished to purchase him from the Indians, but the old man would not give his consent. The traders told Tanner he must go along with his captors, but they promised to follow in about ten days and rescue him. Nothing ever came of this promise.

Soon after this incident the Indians and their captive came

Ojibway grave house

to Lake Erie. Not even stopping to camp at night, they pressed on to Detroit, where they obtained three horses.

On one of these they placed me, on the others their baggage, and sometimes one, sometimes another of the Indians riding, we traveled rapidly, and in about three days reached Sau-ge-nong, the village to which old Manito-o-geezhik belonged. This village or settlement consisted of several scattered houses. . . . Kish-kau-ko and his father . . . left their horses and borrowed a canoe, in which we at last arrived at the old man's house. This was a hut or cabin built of logs, like some of those in Kentucky. As soon as we landed, the old woman came down to us to the shore, and after Manito-o-geezhik had said a few words to her she commenced crying, at the same time hugging and kissing me, and thus she led me to the house.

Next day they took me to the place where the old woman's son had been buried. The grave was enclosed with pickets, in the manner of the Indians, and on each side of it was a smooth open place. Here they all took their seats; the family and friends of Manito-o-geezhik on the one side, and strangers on the other. The friends of the family had come provided with presents; mukkuks of sugar, sacks of corn, beads, strouding [a coarse kind of cotton], tobacco, and the like. They had not been long assembled when my party began to dance, dragging me with them about the grave. Their dance was lively and cheerful, after the manner of the scalp dance. From time to time as they danced they presented me something of the articles they had brought, but as I came round in the dancing to the party on the opposite side of the grave, whatever they had given me was snatched from me; thus they continued a great part of the day, until the presents were exhausted, when they returned home.

Tanner was given the Indian name Shaw-shaw-wa-ne-ba-se (the Falcon), and kept that name during all the time he lived with the tribes. Although his foster mother tried to protect him, he was badly treated by his captors—kicked, beaten, and often half-starved. He was also told that all his own family had been killed.

When young Tanner had lived with these people for about two years, he was sold to Net-no-kwa, a woman who was then regarded as a principal chief of the Ottawas. One of her sons had died and she wished to replace him with John Tanner, who was about the same age. Of Net-no-kwa, Tanner says:

This woman, who was then advanced in years, was of a more pleasing aspect than my former mother. She took me by the hand after she had completed the negotiation with my former possessors and led me to her lodge, which stood near. Here I soon found I was to be treated more indulgently than I had been. She gave me plenty of food, put good clothes upon me, and told me to go and play with her own sons. We remained but a short time at Sau-ge-nong. She would not stop with me at Mackinac, which we passed in the night, but ran along to Point St. Ignace, where she hired some Indians to take care of me while she returned to Mackinac by herself, or with one or two of her young men. After finishing her business at Mackinac she returned and, continuing on our journey, we arrived in a few days at Shab-a-wy-wy-a-gun. The corn was ripe when we reached that place, and after stopping a little while we went three days up the river to the place where they intended to pass the winter. . . .

    The husband of Net-no-kwa was an Ojibway, of Red River, called Taw-ga-we-ninne, the Hunter. He was seventeen years younger than Net-no-kwa and had turned off a former wife on being married to her. Taw-ga-we-ninne was always indulgent and kind to me, treating me like an equal, rather than as a dependent. When speaking to me, he always called me his son. Indeed, he himself was but of secondary importance in the family, as everything belonged to Net-no-kwa, and she had the direction in all affairs of any moment. She imposed on me, for the first year, some tasks. She made me cut wood, bring home game, bring water, and perform other services not commonly required of the boys of my age; but she treated me invariably with so much kindness that I was far more happy and content than I had been in the family of Manito-o-geezhik. She sometimes whipped me, as she did her own children; but I was not so severely and frequently beaten as I had been before.

As Tanner became more expert at hunting and trapping he was gradually relieved of doing domestic chores. Before his first year with Net-no-kwa was over, his foster father was mortally wounded in a fight with another Indian, and his second eldest foster brother, Ke-wa-tin, was gravely injured in a fall. After the death of her husband, Net-no-kwa decided to go to Red River, in Canada. She and the Indians she commanded started on the journey, carrying Ke-wa-tin on a litter whenever it was necessary to take him out of the canoe. At the third carrying place, however, he called a halt, saying "I must die here; I cannot go farther."

Net-no-kwa decided to stop at this place, while the remainder of her party went on. Staying with her were another Indian woman, Net-no-kwa's two sons, and young John Tanner. As Ke-wa-tin was injured, only Tanner and his teen-age foster brother Wa-ma-gon-a-biew were able to hunt for food. It was now summer and they caught fish in the nearby lake and also killed a few beavers, muskrats, and otters. This game, with the corn the Indians had brought along, enabled them to live comfortably.

But, at the approach of winter, the old woman told us she could not venture to remain there by herself, as the winter would be long and cold, and no people, either whites or Indians, near us. Ke-wa-tin was now so sick and weak that in going back to the Portage we were compelled to move slowly; and when we arrived, the waters were beginning to freeze. He lived but a month or two after we arrived. It must have been in the early part, or before the middle, of the winter, that he died. The old woman buried him by the side of her husband, and hung up one of her flags at the grave.

We now, as the weather became severe, began to grow poor, Wa-me-gon-a-biew and myself being unable to kill as much game as we wanted. He was seventeen years of age, and I thirteen, and game was not plentiful.

After Net-no-kwa and her family had lived in a starving condition for some time, a Muskego Indian, hearing of them, took them to his lodge to stay until spring. Here he hunted for them and provided them with everything they needed.

In the spring another man of the same band invited Net-no-kwa's family to hunt with him on a large island in Lake Superior. Here they found an abundance of game. In the fall they returned with their benefactor to Grand Portage. By this time Tanner was allowed a great deal of freedom and might have escaped, but, as he writes:

> I believed my father and all my friends had been murdered, and I remembered the laborious and confined manner in which I must live, if I returned among the whites where, having no friends and being destitute of money or property, I must of necessity be exposed to all the ills of extreme poverty. Among the Indians I saw that those who were too young or too weak to hunt for themselves were sure to find someone to provide for them. I was also rising in the estimation of the Indians and becoming as one of them. I therefore chose, for the present, to remain with them, but always intended at some future time to return and live among the whites.

At about this time, Net-no-kwa's daughter and her three young children joined the family, as Net-no-kwa's son-in-law had been killed. Net-no-kwa decided to go from Grand Portage to Red River, as she had originally planned.

At Red River a large number of Ojibways and Ottawas were encamped and as soon as Net-no-kwa arrived the chiefs met to decide on some way of taking care of her and her family. "These, our relations," said one of the chiefs, "have come to us from a distant country. These two little boys are not able to provide for them, and we must not suffer them to be in want among us." It was agreed that each hunter should give Net-no-kwa's family some share of what he killed.

The Indians had come to this region to trap beaver. They proceeded up the Red River and the Assinneboine to a place called Prairie Portage. Here they left the trader they had brought with them, telling him to wait for them. Here also they abandoned their canoes and walked to a region of small creeks. Tanner and his foster brother were assigned to a creek where there were plenty of beaver and on which only the two boys were allowed to hunt. At first, Tanner was not able to manage the stiff springs of the traps, and whenever he caught a beaver he had to take the whole trap home so that his mother could help him open it. He did well with his trapping, however, and his mother was pleased.

The Indians remained in this place for three months, until game became scarce and they began to suffer from hunger. Taking the advice of the chief man of the band, they decided to move. The day before the removal was a particularly distressing one, with no food, and Net-no-kwa spent that night in loud singing and praying to the Great Spirit. Early the next morning she called Wa-me-gon-a-biew to her and told him that when she finally slept, she dreamed that a man came to her and said, "Net-no-kwa, tomorrow you shall eat bear. There is, at a distance from the path you are to travel tomorrow and in such a direction [which she described to him] a small round meadow with something like a path leading from it; in that path there is a bear."

The woman instructed her son to go to this place, but he had little use for his mother's frequent visionary dreams, and he refused. Tanner, however, could not forget Net-no-kwa's words. After the Indians had arrived at the place where they were to camp for the night, he went back along the way they had come. He turned off the path according to the directions his mother had given.

> At length, I found what appeared at some former time to have been a pond. It was a small, round, open place in the woods, now grown up with grass and some small bushes. This I thought must be the meadow my mother had spoken of; and examining it around, I came to an open place in the bushes, where, it is probable, a small brook ran from the meadow; but

the snow was now so deep that I could see nothing of it. My mother had mentioned that when she saw the bear in her dream, she had, at the same time, seen a smoke rising from the ground. I was confident this was the place she had indicated, and I watched long, expecting to see the smoke; but wearied at length with waiting, I walked a few paces into the open place resembling a path, when I unexpectedly fell up to my middle into the snow. I extricated myself without difficulty and walked on; but remembering that I had heard the Indians speak of killing bears in their holes, it occurred to me that it might be a bear's hole into which I had fallen, and looking down into it, I saw the head of a bear lying close to the bottom of the hole. I placed the muzzle of my gun nearly between his eyes and discharged it.

When he was satisfied that the bear was dead, young Tanner tried to lift it from the hole, but was unable to. He returned to camp and told his mother of his adventure. The bear was sent for and since it was the first one Tanner had killed, the whole band of Indians was invited to a feast, as was customary with such "firsts."

Late in December the Indians finally arrived back in Prairie Portage, the place where they had left their trader. Net-no-kwa and her family remained there for some time. Then Pe-shau-ba, a celebrated war chief of the Ottawas, came looking for them, accompanied by two other men. He had heard in his own country of an old Ottawa woman with a family of children and dependents, but no men, who was living in poverty in the Assinneboine region. He immediately recognized Net-no-kwa as a relative.

Soon after this meeting, Net-no-kwa's family started with Pe-shau-ba on the journey to his country. The snow was deep and the going difficult, but the party at last arrived at Pe-shau-ba's small log hut on Clear Water Lake. Here he had been living for some time with the other two men.

Immediately on his arrival, Pe-shau-ba brought out quantities of beaver skins, dried meat, and dressed skins. "We have long been our own squaws," he said to the women, "but we must be so no longer. It must now be your business to dress our skins, dry our meat, and make our moccasins." The women readily

Ojibway women harvesting wild rice

agreed, and Net-no-kwa herself took charge of the work. Tanner
became the hunting companion of Pe-shau-ba, who seemed to
take pleasure in teaching the boy how to improve his skills in
tracking and killing game.

> Just before the leaves began to appear in the spring we started
> with all our peltries, and large quantities of dried meat and
> dried beaver tails, to come down to the trading house on Mouse
> River. In that country there is no birch or cedar fit for making
> canoes, so that we were compelled to make one for our journey
> of green moose skins, which, being sewed together with great
> care, and being stretched over a proper frame, then suffered to
> dry, make a very strong and good canoe; but in warm weather it
> will not last long. In a canoe of this kind, which would carry

nearly half as much as a common Mackinac boat [perhaps five tons] we all embarked with whatever belonged to us, the intention of Net-no-kwa and Pe-shau-ba being to return to Lake Huron.

At Mouse River, both the Northwest Company and the Hudson's Bay Company had trading houses.

Here Pe-shau-ba and his friends began to drink, and in a short time expended all the peltries they had made in their long and successful hunt. We sold one hundred beaver skins in one day for liquor. The price was then six beaver skins for a quart of rum, but they put a great deal of water with it.

After the men had finished their drinking bout they began to make birchbark canoes, intending to continue their journey to Lake Huron. But at this time the Indians of the region were invited by the Mandan tribe to join them in a war against some of their enemies. Pe-shau-ba and his friends and Tanner's foster brother decided to go with the war party. Tanner was left alone with the women and children, and went with them to Lake Winnipeg, where they remained for two months. He supported the family by hunting and also collected a good many beaver skins.

Returning down the Assinneboine River, Net-no-kwa and her family were passing a frequent camping place of the Indians when they saw some stakes in the ground with pieces of birchbark attached to them; on two of the pieces of bark was the figure of a bear and on the other pieces were figures of other animals. Net-no-kwa immediately recognized these figures as the totems of Pe-shau-ba and his companions. The signs had been left to show that Pe-shau-ba had been here and to tell Net-no-kwa where he had gone. By reading the other marks made along with the totems, she was able to find Pe-shau-ba and his friends at a place about two days' journey away. The war party had failed in its purpose and the men had returned and finished work on the birchbark canoes. The region where they now were camped was excellent for hunting, and the two groups stayed here for some time. They then went to the prairies to hunt buffalo.

When snow came, the men and Tanner's foster brother

went away to trap beaver. Young Tanner was again the sole support of the women and children. The men had left a supply of dried buffalo meat, and Tanner soon found that he was able to kill more buffalo. In the spring he and the women made maple sugar. The men came back at this time, bringing many beaver skins and other valuable furs, the result of their winter's work.

Net-no-kwa still wished to return to Lake Huron. When Pe-shau-ba's friends refused to go, the two groups separated. After Net-no-kwa and her family had traveled some distance toward their destination, Tanner's eighteen-year-old foster brother, Wa-me-gon-a-biew, decided that he too did not wish to leave the north country. As Net-no-kwa would not proceed without him, the family headed back toward Red River. At first, food was plentiful and the boys were successful in their beaver trapping. When snow came, however, they began to suffer from hunger. The Indians at Red River helped them until they themselves faced starvation.

Net-no-kwa and her family then went to the fur trader's at Pembina, where they lived for the rest of the winter. The next winter was spent at the Rainy Lake trading house. Here the agent gave the family credit for 120 beaver skins, to be delivered later, and so they were able to buy blankets, clothing, and other necessities.

There followed a long period of roaming during which the men hunted and trapped. The 120 beaver skins to pay off the credit were delivered to the trading agent and there were surplus skins to buy extra goods. But there was frequent hunger, too. At this point Tanner's story becomes a chronicle of several years of shifting friendships and alliances among the Indians as they banded together for hunting, to keep themselves from starvation. Occasionally one of Net-no-kwa's prophetic dreams led to a successful hunt.

After more time had gone by, Net-no-kwa approached Tanner one day.

I readily perceived by her manner that something unusual had passed. Presently she took me to one side, and began to say to me, "My son, you see that I am now become old; I am scarce able to make you moccasins, to dress and preserve all your skins, and do all that is needed about your lodge. You are now about taking your place as a man and a hunter, and it is right you should have someone who is young and strong to look after your property and take care of your lodge. Wa-ge-tote, who is a good man and one respected by all the Indians, will give you his daughter. You will thus gain a powerful friend and protector, who will be able to assist us in times of difficulty, and I shall be relieved from much anxiety and care for our family." Much more she said, in the same strain; but I told her without hesitation that I would not comply with her request. I had as yet thought little of marriage among the Indians, still thinking I should return before I became old, to marry to the whites. At all events, I assured her I could not now marry the woman she proposed to me. She still insisted that I must take her, stating that the whole affair had been settled between Wa-ge-tote and herself, and that the young woman had said she was not disinclined to the match, and she pretended she could do no otherwise than bring her to the lodge. I told her if she did so I should not treat or consider her as my wife.

The matter was finally settled when the young woman married another man.

When Tanner was in his early twenties he went with his foster brother and many other families of Indians to a region where they were to harvest wild rice.

While we were engaged in collecting and preparing the grain, many among us were seized with a violent sickness. It commenced with cough and hoarseness, and sometimes bleeding from the mouth or nose. In a short time many died, and none were able to hunt. Although I did not escape entirely, my attack appeared at first less violent than that of most others. There had been for several days no meat in the encampment; some of the children had not been sick, and some of those who had been sick now began to recover and needed some food. There was but one man besides myself as capable of exertion as I was; and he, like myself, was recovering. We were wholly unable to walk and could scarce mount our horses when they were brought to us by the children. . . . We rode into the plains and were fortunate enough to overtake and kill a bear. . . . We took it home and distributed to every lodge an equal portion. I con-

tinued to get better, and was among the first to regain my
health, as I supposed. In a few days I went out to hunt elk; and
in killing two of them in the space of two or three hours I
became somewhat excited and fatigued. I cut up the meat, and,
as is usual, took home a load on my back when I returned. I ate
heartily of some which they cooked for me, then lay down and
slept; but before the middle of the night I was waked by a
dreadful pain in my ears. . . . The pain became more and more
excruciating for two days, at the end of which time I became
insensible. . . .

I was unconscious of everything that passed until the band
were nearly ready to move from the place where we had been
living. My strength was not entirely gone, and when I came to
my right mind I could walk about. I reflected much on all that
had passed since I had been among the Indians. I had in the
main been contented since residing in the family of Net-no-kwa;
but this sickness I looked upon as the commencement of mis-
fortune, which was to follow me through life. My hearing was
gone, for abscesses had formed and discharged in each ear, and
I could now hear but very imperfectly. I sat down in the lodge
and could see the faces of men, and their lips moving, but knew
not what they said. I took my gun and went to hunt; but the
animals discovered me before I could see them, and if by acci-
dent I saw a moose or an elk, and endeavored to get near him, I
found that my cunning and success had deserted me. I soon
imagined that the very animals knew that I had become like an
old and useless man.

Under the influence of these painful feelings I resolved to
destroy myself, as the only means of escaping the certain misery
which I saw before me.

When the family was ready to move from the wild-rice
region, Tanner told Net-no-kwa to go ahead, and he would
follow with his horse and gun. When everyone had disappeared he
put his gun into his mouth and tried to discharge it. Nothing
happened. He found that it had been unloaded, that his extra
ammunition had been taken, and that his knife was gone. He
surmised that Net-no-kwa had guessed his intention and had
acted to save him. Frustrated, he went to join his foster mother
and brother, who were waiting for him just out of sight. Later,

when he regained his health and hearing, he was ashamed of his
attempt to take his own life. His friends were so considerate as
never to mention the episode to him, although he notes that sui-
cides were not uncommon among the Indians.

Late the next spring an old Indian chief proposed that
Tanner marry his fifteen-year-old daughter. Net-no-kwa did not
like the girl and rejected the idea. Soon after this, Tanner was
standing by his lodge one evening when he noticed an attractive
young woman walking about and smoking. She asked him to
smoke with her, and they talked together. After that, Tanner saw
her often and gradually became attached to her. Of this meeting
he says:

> I mention this because it was to this woman that I was after-
> wards married, and because the commencement of our ac-
> quaintance was not after the usual manner of the Indians.
> Among them, it most commonly happens, even when a young
> man marries a woman of his own band, he has previously had
> no personal acquaintance with her. They have seen each other
> in the village; he has perhaps looked at her in passing, but it is
> probable they have never spoken together. The match is agreed
> on by the old people, and when their intention is made known
> to the young couple they commonly find in themselves no
> objection to the arrangement, as they know, should it prove dis-
> agreeable mutually or to either party, it can at any time be
> broken off.

Not long after Tanner's marriage he joined a war party
going to fight the Sioux, who were the principal enemies of his
tribe.

> I now began to attend to some of the ceremonies of what may
> be called the initiation of warriors, this being the first time I
> had been on a war party. For the first three times that a man
> accompanies a war party the customs of the Indians require
> some peculiar and painful observances from which old warriors
> may, if they choose, be exempted. The young warrior must con-
> stantly paint his face black; must wear a cap or headdress of
> some kind; must never precede the older warriors, but follow
> them, stepping in their tracks. He must never scratch his head
> or any other part of his body with his fingers, but if he is com-

pelled to scratch, he must use a small stick; the vessel he eats or drinks out of, or the knife he uses, must be touched by no other person. In the two last mentioned particulars, the observances of the young warriors are like those the females in some bands use during their earliest periods of menstruation. The young warrior, however long and fatiguing the march, must neither eat nor drink nor sit down by day; if he halts for a moment he must turn his face toward his own country, that the Great Spirit may see that it is his wish to return home again.

At night they observe a certain order in their encampments. If there are bushes where they halt, the camp is enclosed by these stuck into the ground so as to include a square or oblong space, with a passage, or door, in one end, which is always that toward the enemy's country. If there are not bushes, they mark the ground in the same manner, with small sticks, or the stalks of the weeds which grow in the prairie. Near the gate, or entrance to this camp, is the principal chief and the old warriors; next follow in order, according to age and reputation, the younger men; and last of all, in the extreme end of the camp, those with blacked faces, who are making their first excursion.

In crossing the prairies the war party encountered such hardship that many of the Indians defected. Finally the expedition was given up and the warriors returned home.

A short time later, Tanner ventured into the borderlands of the Sioux country to trap beaver. Here he met an American trader who urged him to leave the Indians and go with him to the states. The trader said that some of Tanner's relatives had been as far as Mackinac in search of him. Tanner preferred to stay with the Indians, for the present, but he thought more frequently of returning to his people and he listened to the advice of an Indian whom he met.

He [the Indian] had in the course of his long life been much among the whites and was well acquainted with the different methods of subsistence among them. He told me that I would be much better situated among the whites, but that I could not become a trader as I was unable to write. I should not like to submit to constant labor, therefore I could not be a farmer. There was but one situation exactly adapted to my habits and qualifications, that of an interpreter. . . .

Shortly after this, we were so reduced by hunger that it was thought necessary to have recourse to a medicine hunt. Nah-gitch-e-gum-me sent to me and O-ge-mah-we-ninne, the two best hunters of the band, each a little leather sack of medicine, consisting of certain roots pounded fine and mixed with red paint, to be applied to the little images or figures of the animals we wished to kill. Precisely the same method is practiced in this kind of hunting, at least as far as the use of medicine is concerned, as in those instances where one Indian attempts to inflict disease or suffering on another. A drawing, or a little image, is made to represent the man, the woman, or the animal on which the power of the medicine is to be tried; then the part representing the heart is punctured with a sharp instrument if the design be to cause death, and a little of the medicine is applied. . . . We started with much confidence of success, but Wah-ka-zhe followed, and overtaking us at some distance, cautioned us against using the medicine Nah-gitch-e-gum-me had given us, as he said it would be the means of mischief and misery to us, not at present, but when we came to die. We therefore did not make use of it, but nevertheless, happening to kill some game, Nah-gitch-e-gum-me thought himself, on account of the supposed efficacy of his medicine, entitled to a handsome share of it. . . .

After I had finished my hunt, and at about the usual time for assembling in the spring, I began to descend the Be-gwi-o-nush-ko to go to the traders at Red River. . . . As I was one morning passing one of our usual encamping places I saw on shore a little stick standing in the bank, and attached to the top of it a piece of birchbark. On examination, I found the mark of a rattlesnake with a knife, the handle touching the snake, and the point sticking into a bear, the head of the latter being down. Near the rattlesnake was the mark of a beaver, one of its dugs, it being a female, touching the snake. This was left for my information and I learned from it that Wa-me-gon-a-biew [Tanner's foster brother], whose totem was She-she-gwah, the rattlesnake, had killed a man whose totem was Muk-kwah, the bear. The murderer could be no other than Wa-me-gon-a-biew, as it was specified that he was the son of a woman whose totem was the beaver, and this I knew could be no other than Net-no-kwa. As there were but few of the bear totem in our band, I was confident the man killed was a young man called Ke-zha-zhoons; that he was dead, and not wounded merely, was indicated by the drooping down of the head of the bear. . . .

The method by which information of this affair was communicated to me at a distance is one in common use among the Indians, and in most cases it is perfectly explicit and satisfactory. The men of the same tribe are extensively acquainted with the totems which belong to each; and if on any record of this kind the figure of a man appears without any designatory mark, it is immediately understood that he is a Sioux, or at least a stranger. Indeed, in most instances, as in that above mentioned, the figures of men are not used at all, merely the totem, or surname, being given. In cases where the information to be communicated is that the party mentioned is starving, the figure of a man is sometimes drawn, and his mouth is painted white, or white paint may be smeared about the mouth of the animal, if it happens to be one, which is his totem.

After visiting the trader on Red River I started with the intention of coming to the states; but at Lake Winnipeg I heard that the war between Great Britain and the United States [the War of 1812] still continued, with such disturbances on the frontier as would render it difficult for me to pass with safety. I was therefore compelled to stop by myself at that place, where I was after some time joined by Pe-shau-ba, Waw-zhe-kah-maish-koon, and others, to the number of three lodges.

Pe-shau-ba, who had befriended Net-no-kwa and her family years before when they were in want, soon became ill and died. Once again, Tanner wished to attempt a journey to the states, but one of the Indians prevented his leaving.

The Hudson's Bay Company no longer had a post in the region. The Northwest Company, the only trading house, was in charge of a Mr. Wells, whom the Indians called Gah-se-moan (the Sail) because he was round and full-bodied. Now that there was no rival trader, Wells announced a new policy toward the Indians. He would no longer give them the credit they usually received in the fall of the year. With that credit they had always bought their winter clothing, ammunition, and often new guns and traps. They were destitute, and it was difficult to see how they could get through the winter without the credit. Tanner protested to Wells, but received no satisfaction.

When winter was half over, Tanner heard that Mr. Hanie, a trader for the Hudson's Bay people, had arrived in the region. Tanner went to him and received all the credit he asked. He had great success with his fur trapping and in the spring sent word to Hanie that he would meet the trader at the mouth of the Assinneboine and pay his credit. Tanner arrived first, and waited for Hanie across the river from the Northwest Company's post. When Wells saw him, he attempted to take Tanner's furs from him by force. An almost murderous fight followed, but Tanner kept his furs, which he paid to Hanie when he arrived. Eventually, Tanner resumed trading with the Northwest Company, but not while Wells was in charge.

Tanner was always a man ready to stand up for his rights and to avenge any slights, real or imagined, against himself. Over the years he appears to have made many enemies. His blue eyes and light complexion were a constant reminder to the Indians that he was not a born tribesman. While many of them considered him a brother, others openly called him an outsider and treated him as such.

Sometimes his quarrels led to serious consequences, as did his differences with an Indian named Ais-kaw-be-wis. This Indian, whom Tanner described as "a quiet, rather insignificant person, a poor hunter," became despondent when his wife died. At length, after living in solitude for a considerable time, he called the chiefs together and announced that he had received a revelation from the Great Spirit. He showed them a ball of clay and said the Great Spirit had spoken to him: "I give you this ball, and as you can see, it is clean and new. I give it to you for your business to make the whole earth like it, even as it was when Na-na-bush first made it. All old things must be destroyed and done away, everything must be made anew, and to your hands, Ais-kaw-be-wis, I commit this great work."

Tanner was indignant at what he felt was Ais-kaw-be-wis' false attempt to represent himself as a chosen messenger of the Great Spirit. Wherever he went, Tanner ridiculed Ais-kaw-be-wis, but many of the Indians believed in this new medicine man. Tanner says:

I now began to experience the inconveniences resulting from having incurred the ill will of Ais-kaw-be-wis. He it was who prejudiced the Indians so much against me, and particularly the relatives of my wife, that my situation at Me-nou-zhe-tau-nang was uncomfortable and I was compelled to return to Red River.

At about this time one hundred or more Scottish people had arrived to settle at Red River under the protection of the Hudson's Bay Company. The agent, Mr. Hanie, employed Tanner to hunt buffalo and furnish the colonists with meat, since they had few provisions. Hanie wished to hire him permanently, but Tanner received a message from his father-in-law asking him to return and live at peace with him. An Indian friend warned that the father-in-law really wished to kill Tanner because Ais-kaw-be-wis had accused him of working bad medicine against several of the family's children and killing them. Tanner decided to return, however, as he felt that his absence would only confirm his father-in-law's suspicions. On his arrival he found the ill will of the Indians so great that he decided to leave them. His wife deserted him and he spent the winter alone with his young children at the hunting grounds. In the spring his wife came back to him. (He had separated from his first wife some years before, and had remarried.)

Soon the Northwest Company called on the Indians to join in an attack on the Hudson's Bay Company's settlement at Red River. Tanner refused to take part, but many of the Indians participated in burning the Red River settlement and in guarding the region to prevent any of the Hudson's Bay people from entering it.

The representatives of the Hudson's Bay Company succeeded in convincing Tanner that right was on their side in their differences with the Northwest Company and they induced him to guide an attack party to their rival's trading house at the mouth of the Assinneboine. Tanner had now almost decided to leave the Indian country and go back to the states. In return for his help, the Hudson's Bay people promised to aid him in his journey.

After Tanner helped capture the Northwest Company's post he met with even more enmity among the Indians. Finally a serious quarrel with an Indian long unfriendly to him almost resulted in his death. He knew that his wife's relatives would gladly see him murdered, so after leaving ample provisions for his family he left on the journey southward. It was long and difficult, but Tanner finally reached his brothers and sisters. He could speak very little English and could not read or write at all. Communication with his relatives was not easy, although they were delighted to have him back. His brother induced Tanner to cut his long hair, take off his Indian brooches and ornaments, and dress as the whites did. But Tanner found the white people's clothing and their houses uncomfortable. From time to time his discomfort forced him to resume Indian dress and sleep outdoors.

After a while Tanner returned to Indian country in order to bring back his family. Once again, this time with his children, he traveled to Kentucky, but after a time found that he was not contented among his white friends. He had now learned the English language well enough to serve as an interpreter and sought employment with the agents at Mackinac and Sault Sainte Marie. As there were no openings, he went north as a trader with the American Fur Company after placing his children in a school at Mackinac.

Tanner remained fifteen months with the American Fur Company. At the end of this time he went to Red River to try to bring back the children of his first marriage—two daughters and a son. When the band of Indians with whom they were living refused to give them up, officers at the Red River fort helped Tanner win the right to take the children away. His son, who was now old enough to make his own decisions, elected to stay among the Indians.

The mother of the children, Tanner's first wife, wished to accompany him, and he started south with her and the two girls. His former wife had no intention of leaving the Indians, however. She connived with a young Indian man to assassinate Tanner with a poison bullet. The attack was devastating. The bones in one of Tanner's arms were shattered and the bullet entered his chest. His former wife and his daughters fled as he lay near death on a riverbank. Eventually he was rescued by some traders who came upon him. They took him to the Rainy Lake trading post where he was nursed back to health. When he was once again able to fend for himself he worked at Mackinac as an Indian interpreter, then was employed as an interpreter by Henry Rowe Schoolcraft, the Indian agent at Sault Sainte Marie. There Tanner lived for many years.

In 1846 he suddenly disappeared. James Schoolcraft, brother of the agent, had been murdered, and Tanner was suspected of the crime. It was thought that he had fled back to the Indians. A search was made, but no trace of him was found.

Years later, a skeleton was uncovered in a swamp near Sault Sainte Marie; it may have been Tanner's. Eventually another man confessed to the slaying of James Schoolcraft. It is possible that Tanner had knowledge of the crime and was murdered by the guilty man—an unhappy ending to a somewhat unhappy life.

JOHN JEWITT

John Jewitt spent over two years in slavery to the king of one of the coastal tribes of northwestern North America. His *Narrative of the Adventures and Sufferings of John R. Jewitt* is one of the classics among accounts of Indian captivities. It portrays a way of life very different from those of the forest and plains tribes. The Indians who took Jewitt captive subsisted by fishing and whaling and by trading the furs of sea otters and seals. Among these Indians life seems more settled and easier than among the tribes who sometimes had to travel many miles to find food.

Jewitt's father was a blacksmith in Boston, England, where his son was born in 1783. The elder Jewitt was convinced of the value of a good education; he sent young John to a good school to learn Latin, mathematics, and other advanced subjects, in the hope that the boy would eventually enter one of the professions. After his schooling had ended, the son rebelled at being apprenticed to a surgeon, as had been planned. He begged instead to learn his father's trade, which had always fascinated him. His father at last consented and in a short time the boy was uncommonly expert at his work.

About a year after young John left school the family moved to Hull, a busy seaport. Here the elder Jewitt did a great deal of work for the ships that put in to the harbor. Young Jewitt became acquainted with the sailors on board some of the vessels, and their stories aroused a wanderlust in him. In 1802, when he was nineteen years old, the ship *Boston*, from Boston, Massachusetts, arrived to take on a cargo of goods suitable for trading with the Indians on the northwest coast of North America. At that time an active fur commerce, especially in sea otter, was carried on with China. Ships were accustomed to leave England, stop to trade for furs and skins on America's northwest coast, then proceed to China to sell their cargo before returning to America.

The *Boston* was in need of repairs and alterations, and John Jewitt's father was hired to do the work, which was considerable. While the ship was being readied, the *Boston*'s captain, with his first and second mates, became friendly with the Jewitts and spent many evenings at their home. The captain often told of his voyages. At length, noticing John Jewitt's interest in his stories, he offered the young man a position as armorer, or blacksmith, aboard the *Boston* for the voyage to the northwest coast and China. With many misgivings the elder Jewitt finally permitted his son to go.

> The ship having undergone a thorough repair and been well coppered, proceeded to take on board her cargo, which consisted of English cloths, Dutch blankets, looking glasses, beads, knives, razors, etc., which were received from Holland, some sugar and molasses, about twenty hogsheads of rum, including stores for the ship, a great quantity of ammunition, cutlasses, pistols, and three thousand muskets and fowling pieces. . . . On the third day of September, 1802, we sailed from the Downs with a fair wind, in company with twenty-four sail of American vessels, most of which were bound home.

Jewitt set up an iron forge on deck and busied himself with putting the muskets in order and with making daggers, knives, and small hatchets for the Indian trade.

The ship rounded Cape Horn and on March 12, 1803, arrived at Nootka Sound at Vancouver Island on America's northwest coast. It headed up the sound for Nootka, a good bay where the captain had decided to stop for wood and water before

A man and woman of the Nootka Sound

proceeding along the coast to trade. Late at night the *Boston* dropped anchor at its destination.

The next morning several native Indians came out from a nearby village in a canoe. They appeared cordial when they boarded the ship. Jewitt had never before seen Indians and he felt great curiosity about them.

> I was, however, particularly struck with the looks of their king, who was a man of a dignified aspect, about six feet in height and extremely straight and well proportioned; his features were in general good and his face was rendered remarkable by a large Roman nose, a very uncommon form of feature among these people; his complexion was of a dark copper hue, though his face, legs, and arms were on this occasion so covered with red paint that their natural color could scarcely be perceived; his eyebrows were painted black in two broad stripes like a new moon, and his long black hair, which shone with oil, was fastened in a bunch on the top of his head and strewed or powdered all over with white down, which gave him a most curious and extraordinary appearance. He was dressed in a large mantle or cloak of the black sea otter skin, which reached to his knees and was fastened around his middle by a broad belt of the cloth of the country, wrought, or painted, with figures of several

colors; this dress was by no means unbecoming, but on the contrary had an air of savage magnificence. His men were habited in mantles of the same cloth, which is made from the bark of a tree, and has some resemblance to straw matting; these [mantles] are nearly square and have two holes in the upper part large enough to admit the arms—they reach as low as the knees, and are fastened around their bodies with a belt about four inches broad of the same cloth.

Because English and American trading ships frequently visited the coast, the king, whose name was Maquina, had learned enough English words to make himself well understood by the crew of the *Boston*. He remained on board for some time while the captain took him to his cabin for a friendly glass of rum.

For the next few days the crew was busy filling the water casks at springs on shore, taking on wood, and cutting timber for the carpenter to make into spars for the ship. The rigging was overhauled and the sails repaired. During this time, Jewitt went on with his blacksmithing work and made such iron parts as were needed by the crew. The Indians came on board daily, bringing fresh salmon, for which they were given articles from the ship's trading store. Because they prized iron weapons and tools they were particularly attentive to Jewitt and crowded around his forge to watch him work.

On March 19, Maquina was invited to dine with the captain. During the dinner conversation the Indian king mentioned that there were many wild ducks and geese nearby. On hearing this, the captain gave Maquina a double-barreled fowling piece, with which the Indian appeared greatly pleased.

> On the 20th we were nearly ready for our departure, having taken in what wood and water we were in want of.
>
> The next day Maquina came on board with nine pair of wild ducks as a present; at the same time he brought with him the gun, one of the locks of which he had broken, telling the captain that it was *peshak*, that is, bad. Captain Salter was very much offended at this observation, and considering it as a mark of contempt for his present, he called the king a liar, adding other opprobrious terms, and taking the gun from him tossed it indignantly into the cabin and calling me to him said, "John,

this fellow has broken this beautiful fowling piece; see if you can mend it." On examining it, I told him that it could be done.

Knowing that Maquina understood English, Jewitt observed him closely to see how he had taken the captain's remarks. It was obvious from Maquina's facial expression that he was angry, although he said nothing.

On the morning of the 22nd the Indians came on board with salmon as usual, and remained on the ship. About noon, Maquina and some of his chiefs arrived. Maquina had a whistle in his hand and over his face he had a wooden mask representing a wild animal. He was in a cheerful mood; while the Indians entertained their hosts with a variety of dances and tricks he blew his whistle in time to their gestures.

When the captain appeared, Maquina told him that there were numbers of salmon in a nearby cove and suggested that the captain send his men to catch some. The ship was leaving the next day, and the captain thought it an excellent idea to have fresh fish for the voyage. Maquina and his chiefs stayed to dine on board the ship. After dinner Captain Salter sent the chief mate and nine men off to catch fish.

Jewitt went below deck to his workbench to clean some muskets. Shortly afterward he heard great noise and confusion on deck.

> I immediately ran up the steerage stairs, but scarcely was my head above deck when I was caught by the hair by one of the savages, and lifted from my feet; fortunately for me, my hair being short, and the ribbon with which it was tied slipping, I fell from his hold into the steerage. As I was falling, he struck at me with an axe, which cut a deep gash in my forehead, and penetrated the skull, but in consequence of his losing his hold, I luckily escaped the full force of the blow; which otherwise would have cleft my head in two. I fell stunned and senseless upon the floor. How long I continued in this situation I know not, but on recovering my senses the first thing that I did was to try to get up; but so weak was I from the loss of blood that I fainted and fell. I was however soon recalled to my recollection by three loud shouts or yells from the savages, which convinced me that they had got possession of the ship.

Jewitt was terrified and expected to be killed at any moment. Presently, wiping the blood from his eyes, he looked up and saw that the steerage hatch had been shut. Later he learned that Maquina, wishing to prevent further injury to a man with such valuable skills as Jewitt's, had ordered the hatch closed. Jewitt remained in a horrible state of suspense for a long time before Maquina, opening the hatch, called him on deck. So weak he could hardly walk, Jewitt obeyed.

> But what a terrific spectacle met my eyes; six naked savages, standing in a circle around me, covered with the blood of my murdered comrades, with their daggers uplifted in their hands, prepared to strike. . . . The king who, as I have already observed, knew enough of English to make himself understood, entered the circle, and placing himself before me, addressed me nearly in the following words—"John—I speak—you no say no. You say no—daggers come." He then asked me if I would be his slave during my life—if I would fight for him in his battles —if I would repair his muskets and make daggers and knives for him—with several other questions, to all of which I was careful to answer yes. He then told me that he would spare my life, and ordered me to kiss his hands and feet to show my submission to him, which I did.

In the meantime, the other Indians were urging that Jewitt be put to death so that no one would be left to tell the tale of the ship's destruction and so discourage other traders from stopping at Nootka. Maquina remained firm in opposing this idea. At length

> . . . he led me to the quarter deck, where the most horrid sight presented itself that ever my eyes witnessed. The heads of our unfortunate captain and his crew, to the number of twenty-five, were all arranged in a line, and Maquina, ordering one of his people to bring a head, asked me whose it was; I answered, the captain's; in like manner the others were showed me, and I told him the names, excepting a few that were so horribly mangled that I was not able to recognize them.

Jewitt learned that the whole crew, including those who had gone fishing, had been murdered. Maquina ordered him to get the ship under way for Friendly Cove, where the village stood.

The Indians were inexpert crewmen, but they finally sailed into the cove at about eight o'clock in the evening. The ship was run ashore on a sandy beach, and a great celebration began.

Maquina took Jewitt to his house, where the king's nine wives received the young man with sympathy and kindness. Other Indians entered, still clamoring for Jewitt's death. Finally, in a rage, Maquina seized a club and drove them off. During this excitement the king's eleven-year-old son, attracted by Jewitt's appearance, approached him. Jewitt patted him in a friendly manner. When the boy appeared responsive, the young man took him on his knee; cutting the metal buttons from his coat, he tied them around the child's neck. The boy was delighted and refused to leave Jewitt's side.

Maquina was pleased with the young man's attention to his son. When it was time to sleep, he told Jewitt to lie with the boy next to him, as he was afraid that some of the Indians might try to kill the Englishman during the night.

About midnight, an Indian came to tell Maquina that one of the crew was still alive and unharmed aboard the ship. The king told Jewitt that he was determined to kill this man as soon as the sun rose.

> As I was thinking of some plan for his preservation, it all at once came into my mind that this man was probably the sail-maker of the ship, named Thompson, as I had not seen his head among those on deck, and knew that he was below at work upon the sails not long before the attack. The more I thought of it, the more probable it appeared to me, and as Thompson was a man nearly forty years of age and had an old look, I conceived it would be easy to make him pass for my father, and by this means prevail on Maquina to spare his life. Towards morning I fell into a doze, but was awakened with the first beams of the sun by the king, who told me that he was going to kill the man who was on board the ship, and ordered me to accompany him. I rose and followed him, leading with me the young prince his son.

By invoking the love that existed between the king and his little boy, Jewitt persuaded Maquina to save his own so-called father, Thompson. The situation was helped when Maquina recognized the sailmaker and observed that Thompson could make some sails for his canoe.

Now the Indians began to strip the vessel of cargo, sails, and rigging. Thompson and Jewitt were obliged to help, and Jewitt was able to secure the ship's accounts and papers, which he hoped in time to return to their rightful owners. He also took the captain's writing desk, containing paper and implements for writing. When he found a blank account book he decided that if he possibly could he would keep a record of his captivity. Both Jewitt and Thompson were members of the Church of England; they were happy to rescue a Book of Common Prayer, a Bible, and a collection of sermons.

Soon other Indians in the region heard of the capture of the ship. A great number of canoes, filled with Indians of at least twenty tribes, began to arrive. There was dancing and feasting, and the guests were given cloth, muskets, powder, and shot in exchange for the whale blubber, oil, herring spawn, and dried fish and clams that they brought.

This happy time ended when the ship was accidentally set afire by a night plunderer who went aboard with a torch. A great deal of the cargo was lost, to the regret of Thompson and Jewitt, who had hoped to use the ship's provisions. They did take off a box of chocolate and a case of port wine, neither of which the Indians liked. Jewitt also saved his tools, although his anvil and the bellows attached to his forge were lost.

Soon his head wound was sufficiently healed so that he began to work at repairing guns and making bracelets and other small ornaments of copper and steel for the king and his wives. For an anvil he used a large square stone, and he heated his metal in an ordinary wood fire.

When Jewitt was not working for Maquina, the king allowed him to work for himself at making bracelets and other copper ornaments, fish hooks, and daggers. Jewitt traded these to members of visiting tribes or to Maquina's chiefs.

> On these occasions, besides supplying me with as much as I wished to eat, and a sufficiency for Thompson, [they] almost always made me a present of an European garment taken from the ship or some fathoms of cloth, which were made up by my

comrade, and enabled us to go comfortably clad for some time; or small bundles of penknives, razors, scissors, etc., for one of which we could almost always procure from the natives two or three fresh salmon, cod, or halibut; or dried fish, clams, and herring spawn from the stranger tribes.

Unfortunately the Englishmen were not allowed to cook their own food, but had to give it to the Indian women to prepare. It was boiled and served with no salt but with a liberal dousing of whale oil—most unappetizing to Thompson and Jewitt.

Thompson was eager for Jewitt to begin his journal of their captivity. On June 1, Jewitt began his diary. He had managed to make a serviceable ink by boiling blackberry juice with finely powdered charcoal and filtering the mixture through a cloth. New quills for writing were no problem, as there were many crows and ravens along the beach. A large clam shell made a good inkstand.

In keeping his diary, Jewitt was well served by his education. He had learned to express himself in writing and was a better than average observer. His diary became the basis for the vivid narrative of his adventures that was later published.

Jewitt had ample opportunity to experience the Nootka way of life.

The Indians lived in a village of about twenty houses, built nearly in a line. These houses were from thirty-six to forty feet wide, but of varying lengths. The king's dwelling was the longest, measuring about 150 feet, while the smallest houses were about forty feet in length. Each building had a ridgepole and two sloping roofs and was covered with wide planks. The roof planks were not fastened to beams, but were held down by large stones. In a stormy gale the men often had to go up on the roofs and weight them down with still more stones.

Each house had only one entrance. A passage ran through the building from one end to the other, and on either side of it several families lived, each with its own fireplace but with no walls to mark the family space. The fireplaces were made of a number of stones put together. There were no chimneys; when a fire was made, the roof plank above it was moved aside by means of a pole, to let the smoke out.

Interior of a Nootka house

Of the Indians' food, Jewitt writes:

Their mode of living is very simple—their food consisting almost wholly of fish, or fish spawn fresh or dried, the blubber of the whale, seal, or sea cow, mussels, clams, and berries of various kinds; all of which are eaten with a profusion of train [whale] oil for sauce, not excepting even the most delicate fruit, as strawberries and raspberries. With so little variety in their food, no great can be expected in their cookery. Of this, indeed, they may be said to know but two methods, viz., by boiling and steaming, and even the latter is not very frequently practiced by them. Their mode of boiling is as follows: into one of their tubs they pour water sufficient to cook the quantity of provision wanted. A number of heated stones are then put in to make it boil, when the salmon or other fish are put in without any other preparation than sometimes cutting off the heads, tails, and fins, the boiling in the meantime being kept up by the application of the hot stones, after which it is left to cook until the whole is nearly reduced to one mass. It is then taken out and distributed in the [wooden] trays. In a similar manner they cook their blubber and spawn, smoked or dried fish, and in fine, almost everything they eat, nothing going down with them like broth. . . .

In eating they make use of nothing but their fingers, except for the soup or oil, which they lade out with clam shells. Around one of these trays from four to six persons will seat themselves, constantly dipping in their fingers or clam shells, one after the other. The king and chiefs alone have separate trays, from which no one is permitted to eat with them, except the queen, or principal wife of the chief, and whenever the king or one of the chiefs wishes to distinguish any of his people with a special mark of favor, on these occasions he calls him and gives him some of the choice bits from his tray. The slaves eat at the same time, and of the same provisions, faring in this respect as well as their masters, being seated with the family and only feeding from separate trays. . . .

In point of personal appearance the people of Nootka are among the best looking of any of the tribes that I have seen. The men are in general from about five feet six to five feet eight inches in height; remarkably straight, of a good form, robust and strong, with their limbs in general well turned and proportioned excepting the legs and feet, which are clumsy and ill formed, owing no doubt to their practice of sitting on them. . . .

As to the women . . . they are in general very well looking and some quite handsome. Maquina's favorite wife, in particular, who was a Wickinninish princess, would be considered as a beautiful woman in any country. She was uncommonly well formed, tall, and of a majestic appearance; her skin remarkably fair for one of these people, with considerable color, her features handsome and her eyes black, soft and languishing; her hair was very long, thick and black, as is that of the females in general, which is much softer than that of the men; in this they take much pride, frequently oiling and plaiting it carefully into two broad plaits, tying the ends with a strip of the cloth of the country; and letting it hang down on each side of the face.

Though the women . . . make but little use of paint, the very reverse is the case with the men. In decorating their heads and faces they place their principal pride, and none of our most fashionable beaus, when preparing for a grand ball, can be more particular; for I have known Maquina, after having been employed for more than an hour in painting his face, to rub the whole off and recommence the operation anew when it did not entirely please him. The manner in which they paint themselves frequently varies, according to the occasion, but it oftener is the mere dictate of whim. The most usual method is to paint the eyebrows black, in form of a half moon, and the face red in small squares, with the arms and legs and part of the body red; sometimes one half of the face is painted red in squares, and the other black; at others, dotted with red spots, or red and black instead of squares, with a variety of other devices, such as painting one half of the face and body red, and the other black. But a method of painting which they sometimes employed, and which they were much more particular in, was by laying on the face a quantity of bear's grease of about one-eighth of an inch thick; this they raised up into ridges resembling a small bead in joiner's work, with a stick prepared for the purpose, and then painted them red, which gave the face a very singular appearance. On extraordinary occasions the king and principal chiefs used to strew over their faces, after painting, a fine black shining powder, procured from some mineral, as Maquina told me it was got from the rocks. This they call *pelpelth*, and value it highly as, in their opinion, it serves to set off their looks to great advantage, glittering, especially in the sun, like silver. This article is brought them in bags by the Newchemass, a very savage nation who live a long way to the north, from whom they likewise receive a superior kind of red paint, a species of very fine and rich ochre, which they hold in much estimation. . . .

In dressing their heads on occasion of a festival or visit, they are full as particular, and almost as long, as in painting. The hair, after being well oiled, is carefully gathered upon the top of the head and secured by a piece of pine or spruce bough with the green leaves upon it. After having it properly fixed in this manner, the king and principal chiefs used to strew all over it the white down obtained from a species of large brown eagle, which abounds on this coast, which they are very particular in arranging so as not to have a single feather out of place, occasionally wetting the hair to make it adhere. This, together with the bough, which is sometimes of considerable size, and stuck over with feathers by means of turpentine [pitch from fir trees], gives them a very singular and grotesque appearance, which they, however, think very becoming, and the first thing they do on learning the arrival of strangers is to go and decorate themselves in this manner.

The men also wore bracelets of painted leather or copper, and large copper earrings. Their most prized adornment was a nose ornament. The middle segment of the nose was pierced when they were children, and the size of the hole was gradually enlarged. Through this hole the common people stuck a smooth round stick that sometimes projected eight or nine inches beyond the face on either side. The king and chiefs wore conical shells or ornaments of copper or brass, suspended by a wire through the nose hole. Jewitt made many of these nose adornments in the shape of hearts and diamonds.

The Indians of Nootka were not forest hunters, but pursued seals, sea otters, and whales. The sea otters were particularly prized because their fur was valuable in the trade with China and could be sold to the visiting trading vessels.

The Indians were accomplished fishermen and skillful whale hunters.

This [the whale] they kill with a kind of javelin or harpoon, thus constructed and fitted. The barbs are formed of bone which are sharpened on the outer side and hollowed within for the purpose of forming a socket for the staff; these are then secured firmly together with whale sinew, the point being fitted so as to receive a piece of mussel shell which is ground to a very sharp edge and secured in its place by means of turpentine. To this head or prong is fastened a strong line of whale sinew about nine feet in length, to the end of which is tied a bark rope from fifty to sixty fathoms long, having from twenty to thirty sealskin floats or buoys attached to it at certain intervals, in order to check the motion of the whale and obstruct his diving. In the socket of the harpoon a staff or pole of about ten feet long, gradually tapering from the middle to each end, is placed: this

Twentieth-century Nootka Indian ready for a whale hunt

the harpooner holds in his hands in order to strike the whale, and immediately detaches it as soon as the fish is struck. The whale is considered as the king's fish, and no other person, when he is present, is permitted to touch him until the royal harpoon has first drawn his blood, however near he may approach; and it would be considered almost a sacrilege for any of the common people to strike a whale before he is killed, particularly if any of the chiefs should be present. They also kill the porpoise and sea cow with harpoons, but this inferior game is not interdicted the lower class.

The people of Nootka made some of the handsomest canoes to be found among the coastal Indians. They were fashioned of pine trees hollowed out with chisels. The outside surface was burned and rubbed down until it was glass-smooth. In this way the exterior was made black, while the inside was painted bright red. The prows and sterns were almost always ornamented with carved figures of ducks or other birds—perhaps a duck's head at the prow, and its tail at the stern. Some canoes, particularly those used in whaling, were also ornamented with two parallel lines of small white shells, placed about two inches below the gunwale. The war canoes were decorated on the outside with figures of eagles, whales, and human heads, painted with a mixture made from white chalk.

The Nootka king and chiefs considered their slaves—both men and women—to be their most valuable property. These slaves were either captured in war or purchased from neighboring tribes. They lived in the same house as their masters and were usually treated as family members, although they were made to work hard, bringing water, cutting wood, making canoes, building houses, fishing, and fighting for their masters during wars.

Though they were slaves, Jewitt and Thompson did not fare badly. They did suffer from constant anxiety that no ship would come to rescue them. Their chief consolation was to go on Sundays to the border of a beautiful little fresh-water lake about a mile from the village. Here they bathed, put on clean clothes, read from the Bible and the Book of Common Prayer, and uttered their own prayers for deliverance.

On the third of September the whole tribe quitted Nootka, according to their constant practice, in order to pass the autumn and winter at Tashees and Cooptee, the latter lying about thirty miles up the sound in a deep bay, the navigation of which is very dangerous from the great number of reefs and rocks with which it abounds. On these occasions everything is taken with them, even the planks of their houses, in order to cover their new dwellings. To a European, such a removal exhibits a scene quite novel and strange; canoes piled up with boards and boxes, and filled with men, women, and children of all ranks and sizes, making the air resound with their cries and songs.

Jewitt and Thompson left Nootka reluctantly, as no ships ever visited the part of the coast to which they were going. The chief reason for the removal was that the Indians could get their winter stock of food at these new sites. There were salmon and salmon spawn, herring and sprats and herring spawn in abundance. The salmon were caught in weirs and many of them were dried for winter use.

While they were in their winter quarters, Maquina told Jewitt that his attack on the *Boston* was only partly in revenge for the captain's treatment. Maquina said that several sea captains had treated him badly, stealing furs, killing his chiefs, and firing on his canoes. Jewitt knew of the bad behavior of some of the captains and crews and could not help but agree that the Indians were justified in rebelling. He felt that if the visiting traders treated the native people with civility they would meet with no trouble.

On February 25 the Indians left Cooptee to return to Nootka. Thompson and Jewitt were happy with the move, as they hoped that during the summer a trading vessel might arrive.

Several chiefs had tried to purchase Jewitt, particularly after they had seen an iron harpoon he made for Maquina. The king refused to part with his blacksmith. During the summer, Ulatilla, chief of the Klaizzarts, arrived at Nootka. To Jewitt he seemed more congenial than any of the other Indians. He spoke English well and liked to talk to Jewitt about England and its customs. He too tried to purchase the blacksmith and told Jewitt that if he was successful he would put him on the first trading ship that arrived in the sound. Maquina still refused to sell his slave. Ulatilla went on his way, after accepting a letter from Jewitt for delivery to the first trading ship the chief encountered. During his captivity, Jewitt wrote sixteen of these letters and gave them to various visiting Indians, but only one of the letters ever reached an American or European vessel.

No ship arrived at Nootka during the summer, and in September the Indians once again left for their winter quarters. Soon after their arrival at Tashees, Maquina told Jewitt that he and his chiefs had decided that the blacksmith must marry one of the Indian women. Maquina said that it was unlikely that Jewitt would ever be rescued and that the sooner he settled down and conformed to Nootka customs, the better. A wife and family would make him more contented with the Indian way of life.

Jewitt protested this decision. When he was told that if he refused to abide by it both he and Thompson would be put to death, he reluctantly agreed. Since he did not fancy any of the Nootka women, he asked permission to make his choice from some other tribe.

The suggestion was agreeable to Maquina. The next morning at daybreak he set off with Jewitt and about fifty other men in two canoes, bound for a village about a day's journey away. In the canoes were cloth, muskets, sea otter furs, and other valuables for the purchase of a bride.

Once the visitors had been allowed to land at their destination, they were invited to a feast of herring spawn and oil. During the festivities Maquina asked Jewitt if he saw any woman whom he liked. Jewitt pointed out a young woman about seventeen years old, the daughter of Upquesta, a chief. After ceremonies during which the virtues of both Jewitt and the girl were praised and the gifts were displayed, the chief consented to the marriage. The next morning the visitors, with the bride, returned to Tashees, where they were joyfully received.

Maquina assigned me as an apartment the space in the upper part of his house, between him and his elder brother, whose room was opposite. Here I established myself with my family, consisting of myself and wife, Thompson, and the little Sat-sat-sak-sis [the king's young son], who had always been strongly attached to me and now solicited his father to let him live with me, to which he consented. This boy was handsome, extremely well formed, amiable, and of a pleasant, sprightly disposition. I used to take a pleasure in decorating him with rings, bracelets, ear jewels, etc., which I made for him of copper, and ornamented and polished them in my best manner. I was also very careful to keep him free from vermin of every kind, washing him and combing his hair every day. . . .

In making my domestic establishment I determined, as far as possible, to live in a more comfortable and cleanly manner than the others. For this purpose I erected with planks a partition of about three feet high, between mine and the adjoining rooms, and made three bedsteads of the same, which I covered with boards, for my family to sleep on, which I found much more comfortable than sleeping on the floor amidst the dirt.

Jewitt describes his young wife as very pretty, amiable, intelligent, neat, clean, and anxious to please. Fond as he was of her, he could not help but view her as a chain that would bind him to the Indians and prevent his ever returning home. His unhappiness increased when, a few days after his marriage, Maquina told him the chiefs' latest decision. Now that Jewitt had married one of the Indian women, he would have to conform to Indian customs. In the future neither he nor Thompson would be allowed to wear their European clothes, but would have to dress like the Indians. This decision was a blow to Jewitt, as the Indians' clothing was not as warm as his own. He did persuade Maquina not to compel Thompson to dress differently, arguing that such a change might cause the older man's death.

Without his customary clothing, Jewitt suffered from the cold. On February 20 the Indians returned to Nootka where, on March 16, he was taken ill with what he describes as a "violent colic." He attributed it to exposure to the cold weather. His illness was painful and he soon became weak. His wife did what she could to help him, but finally Maquina told Jewitt that if living with her made him so ill and sad, he might part with her. Jewitt accepted this proposal and the girl was sent back to her father although she begged to remain. Jewitt himself would have felt sorry to see her go if he had not considered her an obstacle to his possible escape. After she left, Maquina permitted him to change back to European dress. Warmer and more comfortable in his customary clothing, Jewitt began to recover.

Midsummer came, and Thompson and Jewitt were losing hope of a ship's coming to Nootka that season. Then,

> . . . on the morning of the nineteenth of July, a day that will be ever held by me in grateful remembrance of the mercies of God, while I was employed with Thompson in forging daggers for the king, my ears were saluted with the joyful sound of three cannon, and the cries of the inhabitants, exclaiming, Weena, weena—Mamethlee—that is, strangers—white men.

Soon after, several of our people came running into the house to inform me that a vessel under full sail was coming into the harbor. Though my heart bounded with joy, I repressed my feelings, and affecting to pay no attention to what was said, told Thompson to be on his guard and not to betray any joy, as our release, and perhaps our lives, depended on our conducting ourselves so as to induce the natives to suppose we were not very anxious to leave them.

Presently Maquina appeared. He seemed surprised to see the two men at work and asked Jewitt if he did not know that a ship had arrived. Jewitt answered that it was nothing to him. Maquina replied that he had called a council of his people to determine what should be done with the two Englishmen, and they must be present at the meeting.

Of the men assembled at Maquina's house, some wanted to kill Thompson and Jewitt; others suggested that they be hidden until the ship departed. Several of the chiefs wished to release them, but Maquina would not agree to this.

Maquina had a strong desire to go on board the ship, but the other Indians protested, telling him that the captain would kill him or keep him prisoner because he had destroyed the *Boston* and its crew. Finally Maquina asked Jewitt to write a letter, telling the captain that Maquina had treated his captives kindly. Seeing his chance for escape, Jewitt agreed. Instead of the letter Maquina suggested, he wrote the captain to seize Maquina and hold him, so that Jewitt might obtain the release of himself and his companion.

On board the ship, Maquina gave the letter and a present of skins to the captain. He was invited into the cabin and served some crackers and a glass of rum, then he was seized and held prisoner.

When the men on shore learned what had happened, they threatened to kill the two Englishmen. Jewitt was confident that he and Thompson were safe as long as Maquina was held on the ship. He told the Indians that Maquina would be imprisoned only until he and Thompson were released and he suggested that the Indians send Thompson aboard, asking that the captain treat Maquina well. At first, Thompson objected to leaving Jewitt alone on shore, but the younger man reassured him.

When Thompson was safe on board the ship, Jewitt suggested that the Indians take him out in a canoe and hail the captain, asking him to send Maquina in a boat so that an exchange of captives could be made between ship and shore.

Jewitt wished to obtain the *Boston*'s property, which still remained with the Indians. In order to do this, he was determined to get on board the ship before Maquina was released. As the canoe came within hailing distance of the vessel he drew two pistols and ordered the Indians to keep going if they did not wish to be shot. In a few minutes he was aboard the ship.

The captain, Samuel Hill, of the brig *Lydia*, of Boston, Massachusetts, welcomed Jewitt and told him he had heard of his plight through a letter delivered at Klaizzart by the chief Ulatilla. This chief was the one whom Jewitt had particularly liked.

Jewitt had a bearskin wrapped around him, his face was painted, and his long hair was fastened in a large bunch on the top of his head by a sprig of green spruce. Captain Hill later told him he had never seen anything "in the form of man" look so wild as Jewitt had when he first came aboard.

Captain Hill asked the particulars of the *Boston*'s destruction and gave his opinion that Maquina ought to be killed. Jewitt pleaded Maquina's case, saying that he had suffered at the hands of the sailing captains. He asked Hill to keep Maquina a prisoner until the next day, however, when he would try to recover the *Boston*'s property.

The next morning Jewitt hailed the Indians and asked them to bring out the *Boston*'s cannon, anchors, and whatever remained of the cargo. Within two hours everything, including the ship's papers and Jewitt's and Thompson's chests, had been delivered to the *Lydia*, and Maquina was released. He presently returned with about sixty skins for the captain, in gratitude for sparing his life. He further agreed to save whatever skins he should get, to trade with the ship when it came back down the coast in November. Maquina said good-by to Jewitt with great emotion. Jewitt, happy as he was to be free, felt a painful regret at leaving this man who had been kind to him and whom he liked.

Four or five months later, when the *Lydia* returned to Nootka, Maquina delivered the promised skins and told Jewitt that his young wife had given birth to a son, now about five months old. Maquina promised to take the boy when he was older and raise him as his own child. (Apparently Jewitt never made any attempt to see his son.)

The *Lydia* proceeded along the coast until August, 1806, when it left for China. By chance, in Canton, Jewitt met an old acquaintance. He was John Hill, the mate on an English ship. This young man's father had been Jewitt's next-door neighbor in Hull. Hill was startled to see Jewitt, as he had supposed him dead.

> He supplied me with a new suit of clothes and a hat, a small sum of money for my necessary expenses, and a number of little articles for sea stores on my voyage to America. I also gave him a letter for my father, in which I mentioned my wonderful preservation, and escape through the humanity of Captain Hill, with whom I should return to Boston. This letter he enclosed to his father, by a ship that was just sailing, in consequence of which it was received much earlier than it otherwise would have been.

The *Lydia* left China in February, 1807, and arrived in Boston 114 days later. Jewitt found it impossible to express his feelings at being once more in a land where people seemed like himself and spoke his language.

He did not return to England. For a while he remained in Boston, where he published the diary of his captivity. Later he married and went to live in Middletown, Connecticut. There Richard Alsop, a merchant and writer, became interested in Jewitt's adventures. Using the diary and the former captive's oral recollections, Alsop wrote down the narrative *The Adventures and Sufferings of John R. Jewitt*. The book became a best seller of its day. Two years after its publication a play based on its story was produced in Philadelphia, with Jewitt playing the leading role— one he had actually lived. For a time he peddled his book throughout the northeastern part of the United States, where he became a well-known personage. He died in Hartford, Connecticut, in 1821.

FANNY KELLY

Fanny Kelly was born in Orillia, Canada, in 1845. In 1856, when she was eleven years old, her father, James Wiggins, joined a group of New York pioneers going west to Kansas. There they settled in Geneva. Wiggins returned east for his family, but lived only long enough to take them as far as the Missouri River, where he died of cholera. His wife went on to their new home, and there Fanny lived until she was nineteen.

She had been married to Josiah Kelly of Geneva for less than a year when he decided to go farther west, to Idaho. On May 17, 1864, the Kellys with their adopted ten-year-old daughter Mary—Fanny's sister's child—and two black servants started out with a friend, Gardner Wakefield. A few days later they were joined by a Mr. Sharp, a Methodist clergyman. Two or three weeks later they overtook a large wagon train and found among its members a family with whom they were acquainted, Mr. and Mrs. Larimer and their eight-year-old son. The Larimers preferred to travel with a smaller group and joined the Kellys, as did a Mr. Taylor.

The little wagon train was attacked by the Sioux and Fanny

An Indian attack on the plains—painted by Wilden M. Cary

Kelly was captured on July 12, 1864. She spent five months among the Indians. During that time she was able to keep some record of her daily life; she seems to have had a good eye for detail and a more than ordinary appreciation of the natural beauty of a landscape. Her language is somewhat flowery, but she gives the reader an unforgettable picture of the splendor and vastness of the still-unsettled West, with its almost unbelievably varied plant and animal life.

Fanny Kelly had the typical biases of her day; she was firmly convinced of the superiority of her own people. Yet, finding herself alone among the Indians, she made every effort to please them. In return she found friendliness and a respect for her person.

She starts her account of her experiences by describing the carefree days of westward travel that preceded her capture.

The hours of noon and evening rest were spent in preparing our frugal meals, gathering flowers with our children, picking berries, hunting curiosities, or gazing in rapt wonder and admiration at the beauties of this strange, bewildering country.

Our amusements were varied. Singing, reading, writing to friends at home, or pleasant conversation, occupied our leisure hours.

So passed the first few happy days of our emigration to the land of sunshine and flowers.

When the sun had set, when his last rays were flecking the towering peaks of the Rocky Mountains, gathering around the campfires, in our homelike tent, we ate with a relish known only to those who, like us, scented the pure air and lived as nature demanded. . . .

A fine bridge crosses the Kansas River. A half-hour's ride through the dense heavy timber, over a jet-black soil of incalculable richness, brought us to this bridge, which we crossed.

We then beheld the lovely valley of the prairies, intersecting the deep green of graceful slopes, where waves tall prairie grass, among which the wild flowers grow.

Over hundreds of acres these blossoms are scattered, yellow, purple, white, and blue, making the earth look like a rich carpet of variegated colors; those blooming in spring are of tender, modest hue, in later summer and early autumn clothed in gorgeous splendor. . . .

The sky is of wonderful clearness and transparency. Narrow belts and fringes of forest mark the way of winding streams.

In the distance rise conical mounds, wrapped in the soft veil of dim and dreamy haze. . . .

We crossed the Platte River by binding four wagon boxes together, then loaded the boat with goods, and were rowed across by about twenty men. We were several days in crossing. Our cattle and horses swam across. . . .

The day on which our doomed family were scattered and killed was the 12th of July, a warm and oppressive day. The burning sun poured forth its hottest rays upon the great Black Hills and the vast plains of Montana, and the great emigrant road was strewed with men, women, and children, and flocks of cattle, representing towns of adventurers. . . .

Our journey had been pleasant but toilsome, for we had been long weeks on the road.

Slowly our wagons wound through the timber that skirted

the Little Box Elder, and crossing the stream, we ascended the opposite bank.

We had no thought of danger or timid misgivings on the subject of savages, for our fears had been all dispersed by constantly received assurances of their friendliness. At the outposts and ranches we heard nothing but ridicule of their pretensions to warfare, and at Fort Laramie, where information that should have been reliable was given us, we had renewed assurances of the safety of the road and friendliness of the Indians. . . .

We wended our way peacefully and cheerfully on, without a thought of the danger that was lying like a tiger in ambush in our path.

Without a sound of preparation or a word of warning, the bluffs before us were covered with a party of about two hundred and fifty Indians, painted and equipped for war, who uttered the wild warwhoop and fired a signal volley of guns and revolvers into the air.

This terrible and unexpected apparition came upon us with such startling swiftness that we had not time to think before the main body halted and sent out a part of their force, which circled us round at regular intervals, but some distance from our wagons. Recovering from the shock, our men instantly resolved on defense, and corralled the wagons. . . .

Fanny Kelly, however, begged her husband to try to conciliate the Indians, as the people in the wagon train were greatly outnumbered. Kelly went forward to meet the chief and ask his intentions. This man was Ottawa, a war chief of the Oglala band of the Sioux nation. At first the Indians pretended friendship. They asked to exchange one of their horses for the one Kelly was riding, a favorite racehorse. Reluctantly Kelly agreed. The Indians then requested flour and clothing, which they were given. At last they suggested that the little emigrant train go on its way, but when Kelly perceived that they were being led into a rocky glen from which it would be impossible to escape if the Indians attacked, he called a halt. He and the other men decided to prepare a feast for the Indians.

Preparations for supper were under way when the Indians attacked. Sharp, Taylor, and one of the servants were killed outright, and Wakefield was badly wounded. Kelly and the other servant were some distance from the wagons, gathering firewood; the two men escaped, as did Mr. Larimer.

The Indians quickly sprang on the wagons, breaking open trunks and boxes and distributing the goods among themselves. The two women and their children watched in terror. Mrs. Larimer expressed indignation that her husband and Kelly had escaped and left their wives to the Indians, but Mrs. Kelly knew that perhaps the only hope of rescue lay in the two men's speedily getting help. In the meantime, darkness was coming on, and the captives were still uncertain of their fate.

> The first intimation we had that our immediate massacre was not intended was a few articles of clothing presented by a young Indian whose name was Wechala, who intimated that we would have need for them. . . .
>
> From among the confused mass of material of all kinds scattered about, the same young Indian, Wechala, brought me a pair of shoes; also a pair of little Mary's. He looked kindly as he laid these articles before me, intimating by his gestures that our lives were to be spared, and that we should have need of them and other clothing during our long march into captivity. He also brought me some books and letters, all of which I thankfully received.

Fanny Kelly concealed as many as possible of the books and letters in her clothing. If the captives were forced to travel to the Indians' country, she planned to drop these possessions at intervals along the way. They might prove a guide to rescuers or, if an opportunity for escape came, they might help the captives retrace their steps.

Finally the Indians finished loading their horses with plunder from the wagon train, burned what was left, and started northward with their captives. At first the Indians put Fanny Kelly on a crippled horse, which fell, pinning her underneath it and causing her great pain. There was a delay while another horse was saddled. This time, Fanny Kelly and her daughter, Mary, rode on one horse.

> In the darkness of our ride I conceived a plan for the escape of little Mary.
>
> I whispered in her childish ear, "Mary, we are only a few

miles from our camp, and the stream we have crossed you can easily wade through. I have dropped letters on the way, you know, to guide our friends in the direction we have taken; they will guide you back again, and it may be your only chance of escape from destruction. Drop gently down, and lie on the ground for a little while, to avoid being seen; then retrace your steps, and may God in mercy go with you. If I can, I will follow you."

Watching the opportunity, I dropped her gently, carefully, and unobserved to the ground, and she lay there, while the Indians pursued their way, unconscious of their loss.

Presently Mrs. Kelly, too, slipped from her horse, which went on without a rider. The Indians soon discovered her absence, and forming in a line of forty or fifty abreast, they went back over the ground until they found her crouching in the undergrowth.

I told them the child had fallen asleep and dropped from the horse; that I had endeavored to call their attention to it, but in vain; and fearing I would be unable to find her if we rode further, I had jumped down and attempted the search alone.

The Indians used great violence toward me, assuring me that if any further attempts were made to escape, my punishment would be accordingly.

They then promised to send a party out in search of the child when it became light. . . .

Next morning I learned, by signs, that Indians had gone out in search of little Mary, scattering themselves over the hills, in squads. . . .

That day the Indians and their captives traveled until sunset, then camped for the night in a secluded valley. The next morning, Fanny Kelly found that Mrs. Larimer and her son had escaped. A horrible sense of isolation and horror seized her, but she had no course except to proceed with the Indians. She had been given an unruly horse to lead, and her arms were full of various pieces of baggage. Finally, in disgust, she threw away one of these pieces, the pipe of the old chief, a clay tube about three feet long.

That night, when the pipe could not be found, she admitted that she had lost it. The chief, furious, demanded her death, since the pipe was a venerated object, valuable as a peace offering. The Indians were about to place her on an untamed horse and shoot at her when she remembered the money in her pocket. Snatching out her purse, she distributed its contents— $120—among the Indians, and so saved her life.

Camp the next night was by a stream called Powder River. Leaving Powder River, the Indians passed through pine forests and through valleys green with beautiful grasses. Mrs. Kelly continued to drop papers along the way, but now with little hope of their being found. On the sixth night, she attempted to escape into the darkness surrounding the camp, but the ever watchful chief grasped her wrist and pulled her back. About this time, she became the center of a dispute.

> My feet were covered with a pair of good shoes, and the chief's brother-in-law gave me a pair of stockings from his stores, which I gladly accepted, never for a moment suspecting that, in doing thus, I was outraging a custom of the people among whom I was.
>
> The chief saw the gift and made no remark at the time, but soon after he shot one of his brother-in-law's horses, which he objected to in a decided manner, and a quarrel ensued. . . .
>
> The chief would brook no interference, nor would he offer any reparation for the wrong he had inflicted. His brother-in-law, enraged at his arrogance, drew his bow and aimed his arrow at my heart, determined to have satisfaction for the loss of his horse.
>
> I could only cry to God for mercy, and prepare to meet the death which had long hung over my head, when a young Blackfoot, whose name was Jumping Bear, saved me from the approaching doom by dexterously snatching the bow from the savage and hurling it to the earth. . . .
>
> The Indian submitted to his intervention so far that he did not draw his bow again, and my suspense was relieved for the time by the gift of a horse from the chief to his brother-in-law, which calmed the fury of the wronged Indian. . . .
>
> On the 21st of July we left camp early, the day being cool and favorable for traveling. Our route lay over rolling prairie, interspersed with extensive tracts of marsh, which, however, we easily avoided crossing. A few miles brought us to a high,

A buffalo hunt—painted by George Catlin

broken ridge, stretching nearly in a north and south direction. As we ascended the ridge we came in sight of a large herd of buffalo, quietly feeding upon the bunch, or buffalo, grass, which they prefer to all other kinds. These animals are short-sighted, and scent the approach of an enemy before they can see him, and thus, in their curiosity, often start to meet him, until they approach near enough to ascertain to their satisfaction whether there be danger in a closer acquaintance. In this case they decided in the affirmative, and when they had once fairly made us out, lost no time in increasing the distance between us, starting on a slow, clumsy trot, which was soon quickened to a gait that generally left most pursuers far in the rear.

But the Indians and their horses both are trained buffalo hunters, and soon succeeded in surrounding a number. They ride alongside their victim, and leveling their guns or arrows, send their aimed shot in the region of the heart, then ride off to a safe distance, to avoid the desperate lunge which a wounded buffalo seldom fails to make, and shaking his shaggy head, crowned with horns of most formidable strength, stands at bay, with eyes darting, savage and defiant, as he looks at his human foe. Soon the blood begins to spurt from his mouth and to choke him as it comes. The hunters do not shoot again, but wait patiently until their victim grows weak from loss of blood, and staggering, falls upon his knees, makes a desperate effort to regain his feet and get at his slayer, then falling once more, rolls over on his side, dead.

Here the Indians made a feast of raw buffalo meat, which, Mrs. Kelly says:

I did not accept, thinking then it would never be possible for me to eat uncooked meat.

They remained there overnight, starting early next morning. We were now nearing the village where the Indians belonged.

Jumping Bear, the young Indian who had shown me so many marks of good will, again made his appearance, with a sad expression on his face, and that day would ride in silence by my side; which was an act of great condescension on his part, for these men rarely thus equalize themselves with women, but ride in advance. . . .

We were now nearing a river, which from its locality, must have been the Tongue River, where we found refreshing drink, and rested for a short time. The Indians gave me to understand that when we crossed the stream, and a short distance beyond, we would be at their home.

Here they paused to dress, so as to make a gay appearance and imposing entrance into the village. Except when in full dress, an Indian's wearing apparel consists only of a buffalo robe, which is also part of a fine toilet. It is very inconveniently disposed about the person, without fastening, and must be held in position with the hands.

Many of the Indians decked themselves out in clothing taken from the wagon train.

Ottawa, or Silver Horn, the war chief, was arrayed in full costume. He was very old, over seventy-five, partially blind, and a little below the medium height. He was very ferocious and savage-looking, and now, when in costume, looked frightful. His face was red, with stripes of black, and around each eye a circlet of bright yellow. His long black hair was divided into two braids, with a scalp lock on top of the head. His ears held great brass wire rings, full six inches in diameter, and chains and bead necklaces were suspended from his neck; armlets and bracelets of brass, together with a string of bears' claws, completed his jewelry. He wore leggings of deerskin, and a shirt of the same material, beautifully ornamented with beads, and fringed with scalp locks that he claimed to have taken from his enemies, both red and white. Over his shoulders hung a great bright-colored quilt that had been taken from our stores. He wore a crown of eagle feathers on his head; also a plume of feathers depending from the back of the crown.

His horse, a noble-looking animal, was no less gorgeously arrayed. His ears were pierced, like his master's and his neck was encircled by a wreath of bears' claws, taken from animals that the chief had slain. Some bells and a human scalp hung from his mane, forming together, thus arrayed, a museum of the trophies of the old chief's prowess on the war path, and of skill in the chase. . . .

The entire Indian village poured forth to meet us, amid song and wild dancing, in the most enthusiastic manner, flourishing flags and weapons of war in frenzied joy as we entered the village which, stretched for miles along the banks of the stream, resembled a vast military encampment, with the wigwams covered with white skins, like Sibley tents in shape and size, ranged without regard to order, but facing one point of the compass.

We penetrated through the irregular settlement for over a mile, accompanied by the enthusiastic escort of men, women, and children.

We rode in the center of a double column of Indians and directly in the rear of the chief, till we reached the door of his lodge, when several of his wives came out to meet him. He had six, but the senior one remained in the tent, while a younger one was absent with the Farmer or Grosventre Indians. Their salutation is very much in the manner of the Mexicans; the women crossed their arms on the chief's breast, and smiled.

They met me in silence, but with looks of great astonishment.

I got down as directed and followed the chief into the great lodge or tent, distinguished from the others by its superior orna-

ments. It was decorated with brilliantly colored porcupine quills
and a terrible fringe of human scalp locks, taken in battle with
the Pawnees. . . .

I was shown a seat opposite the entrance on a buffalo skin.
The chief's spoil was brought in for division by his elderly
spouse.

It soon became evident that there was to be no division.
The senior wife, after viewing the goods seized from the wagon
train, announced that she would keep them all for herself. When
the other wives rebelled, she threatened them with a knife,
saying that she was the oldest and had the right to govern. After
the chief made a speech that quieted the women, he departed to
a feast. Crowds of villagers came in to stare at Mrs. Kelly. She
was surprised to see a number of children with light complex-
ions, and later learned that their mothers were Indian, but their
fathers were white soldiers at Fort Laramie.

> Now that the question of property was decided among the
> women of the chief's family, they seemed kindly disposed
> toward me, and one of them brought me a dish of meat; many
> others followed her example, even from the neighboring lodges,
> and really seemed to pity me, and showed great evidences of
> compassion, and tried to express their sympathy in signs,
> because I had been torn from my own people, and compelled to
> come such a long fatiguing journey, and examined me all over
> and over again, and all about my dress, hands, and feet particu-
> larly. Then, to their great surprise, they discovered my bruised
> and almost broken limbs that occurred when first taken, also
> from the fall of the horse the first night of my captivity, and
> proceeded at once to dress my wounds.

Mrs. Kelly was beginning to relax amid this kindness when a
message came from the chief, saying that she was to accompany
him to several feasts. When she showed fear, the eldest wife
allowed the chief's little daughter Yellow Bird to go along with
her. At the feasts the captive was received with promises of good
will and protection, and the chief told her that henceforth she
might have Yellow Bird in place of her own daughter.

> When at nightfall we returned to the lodge which, they told
> me, I must henceforth regard as home, I found the elder

woman busily pounding a post into the ground, and my fears were at once aroused, being always ready to take alarm, and suggested to me that it betokened some evil. On the contrary, it was simply some household arrangement of her own, for presently, putting on a camp kettle, she built a fire and caused water to boil and drew a tea, of which she gave me a portion, assuring me that it would cure the tired and weary feeling and secure me a good rest.

This proved true. Soon a deep drowsiness began to steal over the weary captive. My bed of furs was shown me. Yellow Bird was told to share my couch with me, and from this time on she was my constant attendant. I laid down, and the wife of the chief tenderly removed my moccasins, and I slept sweetly— the first true sleep I had enjoyed in many weary nights. . . .

The day of the 25th of July was observed by continual feasting in honor of the safe return of the braves. . . .

The next morning the whole village was in motion. The warriors were going to battle against a white enemy, they said, and old men, women, and children were sent out in another direction to a place of safety, as designated by the chief. Everything was soon moving. With the rapidity of custom the tent poles were lowered and the tents rolled up. The cooking utensils were put together and laid on cross-beams connecting the lower ends of the poles as they trail the ground from the horses' sides, to which they are attached. Dogs, too, are made useful in this exodus, and started off, with smaller burdens dragging after them, in the same manner that horses are packed.

The whole village was in commotion, children screaming or laughing; dogs barking or growling under their heavy burdens; squaws running hither and thither, pulling down tipi poles, packing up everything, and leading horses and dogs with huge burdens.

The small children are placed in sacks of buffalo skin and hung upon saddles or their mothers' backs. The wrapped-up lodges, which are secured by thongs, are fastened to the poles on the horses' backs, together with sundry other articles of domestic use, and upon these are seated women and children. To guide the horse a woman goes before, holding the bridle, carrying on her back a load nearly as large as the horse carries. Women and children are sometimes mounted upon horses,

Sioux moving camp—painted by George Catlin

holding in their arms every variety of plunder, sometimes little dogs and other forlorn and hungry-looking pets. In this unsightly manner, sometimes two or three thousand families are transported many miles at the same migration and, all being in motion at the same time, the cavalcade extends for a great distance.

The men and boys are not so unsightly in their appearance, being mounted upon good horses and the best Indian ponies, riding in groups, leaving the women and children to trudge along with the burdened horses and dogs.

The number and utility of these faithful dogs is sometimes astonishing, as they count hundreds, each bearing a portion of the general household goods. Two poles, about ten or twelve feet long, are attached to the shoulders of a dog, leaving one end of each dragging upon the ground. On these poles a small burden is carried, and with it the faithful canine jogs along, looking neither to the right nor to the left, but apparently intent upon reaching the end of his journey. . . .

This train was immensely large, nearly the whole Sioux nation having concentrated there for the purpose of war. The chief's sisters brought me a horse saddled, told me to mount, and accompany the already moving column that seemed to be spreading far over the hills to the northward. We toiled on all day. Late in the afternoon we arrived at the ground of encampment, and rested for further orders from the warriors, who had gone to battle and would join us there.

I had no means of informing myself at that time with whom the war was raging, but afterward learned that General Sully's army was pursuing the Sioux, and that the engagement was with his men.

General Alfred Sully and his troops of the U.S. Army had been sent on a punitive expedition against the Sioux because of their attacks on the whites who were encroaching on Sioux territory.

In three days the Indian men returned. Their feasting and rejoicing indicated to Mrs. Kelly that they had suffered few losses. She felt an understanding of the Indians' attitude toward white settlers.

This country seemed scarred by countless trails, where the Indian ponies have dragged lodge poles in their change of habitations or hunting. The antipathy of the Indians to its occupation or invasion by the white man is very intense and bitter. The felling of timber, or killing of buffalo, or traveling of a [wagon] train, or any signs of permanent possession by the white man excites deadly hostility. It is their last hope; if they yield and give up this, they will have to die or ever after be governed by the white man's laws; consequently they lose no opportunity to kill or steal from and harass the whites when they can do so.

The game still clings to its favorite haunts, and the Indians must press upon the steps of the white man or lose all hope of independence. Herds of elk proudly stand with erect antlers, as if charmed by music, or as if curious to understand this strange inroad upon their long-secluded parks of pleasure; the mountain sheep look down from belting crags that skirt the perpendicular northern face of the mountains, and yield no rival of their charms or excellence for food. The black and white-tail deer and antelope are ever present, while the hare and the rabbit, the sage hen, and the prairie chicken are nearly trodden down before they yield to the intrusion of the stranger.

Brants, wild geese, and ducks multiply and people the

waters of beautiful lakes, and are found in many of the streams. The grizzly and cinnamon bears are often killed and give up their rich material for the hunter's profit; and the buffalo, in numberless herds, with tens of thousands in a herd, sweep back and forth, filling the valley as far as the eye can reach, and adding their value to the red man both for food, habitation, fuel, and clothing. The Big Horn River, and mountains and streams beyond, are plentifully supplied with various kinds of fish. The country seems to be filled with wolves, which pierce the night air with their howls, but, like the beavers, whose dams encumber all the smaller streams, and the otter, are forced to yield their nice coats for the Indian as well as white man's luxury.

The Indians still felt that General Sully's army was too near; on August 8 they went out to fight his troops again. This time the battle came dangerously close to the encampment, and the women and children started moving on, trying to keep out of the line of fire.

> On and still on we were forced to fly to a place known among them as the Bad Lands, a section of country so wildly desolate and barren as to induce the belief that its present appearance is the effect of volcanic action. . . .
>
> The terrible scarcity of water and grass urged us forward, and General Sully's army in the rear gave us no rest.

At last, in great danger from the pursuing army, the Indians abandoned all their possessions except their animals and swam the Yellowstone River. When General Sully and his troops stopped to destroy the abandoned property, the fleeing people gained a day to get beyond his reach.

General Sully's troops withdrew from their pursuit and the Indians started homeward. They were now in a terrible state of poverty and hunger. Their food and belongings had been destroyed and there was no game in the part of the country where they now were. Many of the horses and dogs died of starvation and were immediately eaten by the Indians. Some of the Sioux, blaming the white people for their misfortunes, wanted to burn Fanny Kelly at the stake, but Ottawa spoke of how well liked she had been among them and persuaded the avengers to spare her life.

One very hot day a dark cloud seemed suddenly to pass before the sun and threaten a great storm. The wind rose, and the cloud became still darker until the light of day was almost obscured. A few drops sprinkled the earth and then, in a heavy, blinding, and apparently inexhaustible shower, fell a countless swarm of grasshoppers, covering everything and rendering the air almost black by their descent.

It is impossible to convey an idea of their extent; they seemed to rival Pharaoh's locusts in number, and no doubt would have done damage to the food of the savages had they not fallen victims themselves to their keen appetites.

To catch them, large holes are dug in the ground, which are heated by fires. Into these apertures the insects are then driven, and the fires having been removed, the heated earth bakes them.

They are considered good food, and were greedily devoured by the famishing Sioux. Although the grasshoppers only remained two days, and went as suddenly as they had come, the Indians seemed refreshed by feasting on such small game, and continued to move forward.

Hunger was the cause of another dispute centering around Fanny Kelly. One day when she was faint from starvation a neighboring woman asked her to come share a piece of meat. Ottawa, the chief, also eager for food, followed along. His senior wife was watching and came flying into the neighbor's lodge, brandishing a knife and vowing to kill Mrs. Kelly. In the skirmish that followed, shots were fired. One bullet entered Ottawa's arm, breaking it near the shoulder. Fanny Kelly fled, but was soon sent for to dress his wounds. In the village she had achieved a reputation as a good nurse.

Fanny Kelly never saw the old wife again. After the shooting incident, Mrs. Kelly was required to wait on the disabled chief, and shared a lodge with him and his three sisters, whom she found companionable. At this time, she first learned that she was being sought by her own people.

Before the Indians left this camping ground there arrived among us an Indian called Porcupine. He was well dressed, and mounted on a fine horse, and brought with him presents and valuables that insured him a cordial reception.

After he had been a few days in the village he gave me a letter from Captain Marshall, of the Eleventh Ohio Cavalry, detailing the unsuccessful attempts that had been made to rescue me, and stating that this friendly Indian had undertaken to bring me back, for which he would be rewarded.

The letter further said that he had received a horse and necessary provisions for the journey, and had left his three wives, with thirteen others, at the fort as hostages.

Ottawa found Fanny Kelly a pleasant and useful servant, and he was determined to keep her. Finally Porcupine departed, saying that he would either report her dead or impossible to find. During his time in the village he had spread the news that a large ransom had been offered for her. A few Indians began to seek her out with the intention of gaining the reward. One man worked out a plan for her escape, but a series of misadventures brought it to nothing. Then hope arrived from a different quarter.

On September 5 the Indians surprised a military escort commanded by Captain James Fisk, which was accompanying an emigrant train going westward. Two wagons were captured and fourteen of the emigrants were killed. Captain Fisk had cannons and, instead of moving on, he took a stand where he was. Fearing the cannons, the Indians were anxious for the train to start onward so that they could attack in a way that would give them the advantage.

Fanny Kelly begged to be released to the troops, but was refused. At last she persuaded the Indians to allow her to write a note to Captain Fisk saying that the Indians wanted peace and asking him to proceed on his way. She knew that once the wagon train moved, it would be attacked, so she decided to outwit the Indians. Using the same number of words that they dictated, she warned Fisk not to move and begged him to try to rescue her. The letter was carefully examined by the chief; he could not read the writing, but he did count the number of words. Once he was satisfied that its content was correct, he had the letter carried to a hill in sight of the soldiers' camp and fastened to a pole.

The letter was retrieved by Fisk's men and a reply was put in the same place. Fisk wrote that he distrusted the Indians. The next day Mrs. Kelly was asked to write again, assuring the troops of the Indians' friendship. In order that Fisk might be sure she was a white captive, Fanny Kelly told him she would find an excuse to stand on a certain hill where he could see her with field glasses.

Once the troops were sure who she was, they wanted to rescue her, but Fisk was not equipped for an attack and tried to arrange a ransom. The Indians pretended interest, but among themselves they laughed at the offer. Mrs. Kelly, fearing that any ransom messengers who came to the village would be killed, warned Fisk to give up his efforts for her release. He finally succeeded in getting on his way, and spread the news that he had seen her and communicated with her.

> Captain Fisk had made known to General Sully [at Fort Sully, in Dakota] the fact of my being among the Indians, and the efforts he had made for my release; and when the Blackfeet presented themselves before the general, asking for peace and avowing their weariness of hostility, anxious to purchase arms, ammunition, and necessaries for the approaching winter, he replied:
>
> "I want no peace with you. You hold in captivity a white woman; deliver her up to us, and we will believe in your professions. But unless you do, we will raise an army of soldiers as numerous as the trees on the Missouri River and exterminate the Indians."
>
> The Blackfeet assured General Sully that they held no white woman in their possession, but that I was among the Oglalas.
>
> "As you are friendly with them," said the general, "go to them and secure her, and we will then reward you for so doing."

A few days later, the Blackfeet appeared in the Oglalas' village, but that band refused to give Fanny Kelly up.

> They held solemn council for two days, and at last resolved that the Blackfeet should take me as a ruse, to enable them to enter the fort [Fort Sully], and a wholesale slaughter should exterminate the soldiers.

Some of the Oglalas were still unwilling to have Fanny Kelly go, but the Blackfeet promised to treat her kindly and to return her safely. As a guarantee, they left the Oglalas three of

Blackfeet Indians on horseback—painted by Karl Bodmer

their best horses. Fanny Kelly herself was sorry to leave the chief's sisters, who were her friends, and she disliked leaving the protection of the chief, who had given her security from any "injury or insult," as she writes.

Once at the Blackfoot village, she found that she was indeed treated with great kindness and respect. A constant visitation of Indians began, as various groups tried to win her away and so collect the reward for her. The Blackfeet repulsed all such attempts. The weather was cold and snowy; deep drifts blocked the mountain passes and made a journey to Fort Sully impossible for the time being.

One day, Jumping Bear, the Blackfoot Indian who had saved Fanny Kelly's life in the early days of her captivity, appeared. He reminded her of her indebtedness to him and assured her of his devotion.

Fanny Kelly demanded proof of his friendship and asked him to carry a letter to Fort Sully. When he replied that he did not dare go against the wishes of the other Indians he was assured that the letter would contain nothing that would harm him or his people, but would tell of his kindness. Finally Jumping Bear consented to act as messenger. The letter was in reality a warning to General Sully of the plot to use Fanny Kelly as a means of getting inside the fort. Jumping Bear delivered the message, received a reward, and was given a letter to take to Mrs. Kelly. Instead, he disappeared. As a consequence of her message, the fort was made as secure as possible in every way.

Finally the Blackfeet started on their two-hundred-mile journey to take their captive to Fort Sully. The weather was intensely cold. Fanny Kelly, clothed in a cotton dress, moccasins, and a buffalo robe, suffered greatly, and walked a good part of the way to keep from freezing.

When the fort was reached on December 12 the Indians made ready their weapons; some men were placed in ambush around the walls while the others went forward. Eight chiefs rode in advance, one of them leading Fanny Kelly's horse.

Several officers appeared, to receive the chiefs. As they rode through the gate with Mrs. Kelly the order was given to close it behind them. The main body of warriors was shut out and Fanny Kelly realized in an overpowering rush of delight that the fort was saved and she was free.

Josiah Kelly was not at the fort when his wife arrived. He had spent the time since his escape in trying to effect her rescue or ransom, and was at Leavenworth endeavoring to get further help when he heard she had been freed. He rushed to Fort Sully at once.

One of Fanny Kelly's first inquiries to him was concerning their daughter Mary. Josiah Kelly's story was a sad one. On the night she escaped, Mary had found her way back to the great emigrant road. The next morning, three soldiers who had been to Fort Laramie to meet the paymaster had seen her standing on a bluff above the road. Fearing that she might be a decoy placed by the Indians to lure them into ambush, they would not go near her. When they arrived at Deer Creek Station they told of seeing the girl. Josiah Kelly, arriving soon after, heard of their story and thought the child might be Mary. By the time he was able to persuade some soldiers to accompany him to the bluff, it was too late. He found her arrow-pierced body and saw that she had been scalped. He and his companions buried her body in a grave on the spot where she fell.

Saddened by their experiences, the Kellys returned to Geneva, Kansas, but soon set out again. They settled in Ellsworth, a new town on the western border of Kansas, where they built a hotel and prospered until the Indians threatened again. Southern troops sent to protect the town brought cholera with them. Josiah Kelly died in the epidemic that followed.

Fanny Kelly went on to Wyoming, where she stayed with friends for a year, after which she set out for Washington, D.C., to present a claim for losses sustained at the hands of the Indians. Her story was well known in the capital, and papers on file in the War Department told of her help in saving Captain Fisk's troops from destruction and in warning the officers at Fort Sully of the plot against them. A bill was passed by Congress awarding her $5,000 for her services to the government.

While she was in Washington a number of chiefs of the Dakota and Sioux nations arrived to confer with officials of the Bureau of Indian Affairs. Some of them recognized Mrs. Kelly and seemed glad to see her. She went to several of the meetings between the Indians and the commissioners. At one of these meetings, Red Cloud, a chief, pointed her out, saying that the Indians had robbed her of her belongings and that they wished to compensate her out of the first money they received from the government. They asked her to make out a bill for her losses, which they signed. Once this agreement was completed, Fanny Kelly's experiences with the Indians ended.

BIBLIOGRAPHY

Newberry Library. *Narratives of Captivity among the Indians of North America: a List of Books and Manuscripts on this Subject in the Edward E. Ayer Collection of the Newberry Library.* Chicago: The Newberry Library, 1912.

Jewitt, John R. *The Adventures and Sufferings of John R. Jewitt.* Edited, with an introduction and notes, by Robert Brown. London: C. Wilson, 1896.

Kelly, Fanny. *Narrative of my Captivity among the Sioux Indians.* Cincinnati, Ohio: Wilstach, Baldwin & Co., 1871.

Rowlandson, Mary. *A Narrative of the Captivity, Sufferings, and Removes of Mrs. Mary Rowlandson.* Boston: John Boyle's Printing-Office, 1773.

Seaver, James Everett. *A Narrative of the Life of Mary Jemison, the White Woman of the Genesee.* Revised by Charles Delamater Vail. New York: The American Scenic and Historic Preservation Society, 1925.

Smith, James. *An Account of the Remarkable Occurrences in the Life and Travels of Colonel James Smith, during his Captivity with the Indians.* Philadelphia: J. Grigg, 1831.

Tanner, John. A *Narrative of the Captivity and Adventures of John Tanner (U.S. Interpreter at the Sault Ste. Marie) during Thirty Years Residence among the Indians in the Interior of America.* Prepared for the press by Edwin James. New York: G. & C. & H. Carvill, 1830.

INDEX